Campus Sexual Assault

Campus Sexual Assault

College Women Respond

Lauren J. Germain

JOHNS HOPKINS UNIVERSITY PRESS   BALTIMORE

© 2016 Johns Hopkins University Press
All rights reserved. Published 2016
Printed in the United States of America on acid-free paper
9   8   7   6   5   4   3   2   1

Johns Hopkins University Press
2715 North Charles Street
Baltimore, Maryland 21218-4363
www.press.jhu.edu

Library of Congress Cataloging-in-Publication Data

Germain, Lauren J., 1983–
Campus sexual assault: College women respond / Lauren J. Germain.
     pages cm
   Includes bibliographical references and index.
     ISBN 978-1-4214-1905-3 (hardcover : alk. paper) — ISBN 978-1-4214-1906-0
(electronic) — ISBN 1-4214-1905-X (hardcover : alk. paper) — ISBN 1-4214-1906-8
(electronic)   1. Rape in universities and colleges—United States.   2. Women
college students—Crimes against—United States.   3. Rape victims—
Rehabilitation—United States   4. Rape victims—United States—Psychology.
I. Title.
   LB2345.3.R37G47 2016
   364.15'320973—dc23   2015022720

A catalog record for this book is available from the British Library.

*Special discounts are available for bulk purchases of this book. For more information,
please contact Special Sales at 410-516-6936 or specialsales@press.jhu.edu.*

Johns Hopkins University Press uses environmentally friendly book materials,
including recycled text paper that is composed of at least 30 percent post-consumer
waste, whenever possible.

To the brave individuals who told their stories and to those who bear witness and are moved

Contents

Preface

One evening, many years ago, a courageous young woman shared her story with me. At the time, her narrative was in fragments, pieces of sentences punctuated by long pauses where she searched for the next word. She had been raped at college, although she didn't use those words to describe the experience at the time. My response was likewise splintered because I wasn't sure what to say or do, but I listened and promised to "be there."

Being there has meant bearing witness and working to more deeply understand the issue and impact of campus sexual violence. There is research on the prevalence of such violence and some studies on college women's responses to attacks that focus attention on how rarely cases are brought to hearings and trials. Yet when I spoke to women who attended college, I realized that something major was missing from the academic literature on campus sexual violence: real stories, complete in their fragmentation, that include women's responses to these violations and the motivation behind their actions. In listening to their stories, I came to understand campus sexual violence differently and more fully. As previous research has noted, these are stories about adversity, but they are also about the women's own power and agency. By agency, I mean an extension of Laura Ahearn's definition from one's "socio-culturally mediated capacity to act," to include motivation and action.[1] This book is founded on shared stories and shifts the focus from adversity alone to "agency in adversity."

Campus Sexual Assault is about what women did in the aftermath of campus sexual violence. The process of collecting stories and sharing them was one of collective or shared agency. In simply asking "what *did* you do?" I learned about both diversity and commonality. Most importantly, all of the women who told their stories did so with a goal of increasing awareness and helping others. In reading this book and reflecting on what they say, you too contribute to the accomplishment of this aim.

Deciding how to compile these stories was an exercise of my own agency, and I want to be clear about some of the choices I made. I focused on one campus because collegiate cultures and resources vary and I felt it was important to try to capture many perspectives within one site. However, a national study concluded that sexual assault prevalence rates are not very different based on size or institutional type or setting (urban, rural, etc.). So, while campus cultures do vary, the stories that these women shared are applicable across the board. I believe that the core concepts addressed in the book are common to many universities and colleges and this is supported by data showing that campus sexual violence is prevalent at institutions across the country.[2] I intentionally masked the identity of the campus and the women in the book because of my agreements with the human subjects review board and the women interviewed.

What *does* set the research site apart from other institutions are the administrators, faculty, students, and staff who accepted, supported, and learned from this project. It is not easy to let a researcher talk with students on "your" campus about their experiences with sexual assault, but not only did administrators do so, they asked for feedback and are working to improve support services. Many institutions could learn from the site's acceptance and reflexivity.

I also made deliberate decisions about naming. I call the research site simply "the University" due to agreements made with the institutional review board at the site. In naming the women in the book, I moved forward through the alphabet from A to Z so that the names would not carry meaning but would allow us to refer to different aspects of the narratives. In naming perpetrators, I tried to move backward through the alphabet from Z to A for the same reason.

Finally, when possible, I preserved the ways that women spoke by using their authentic voices. There are unedited quotations throughout the book that may be a bit difficult to read because they are fragmented, include pauses and words that women said while thinking such as "like" and "um," and show changes of direction mid-sentence. Editing these exchanges would have removed the power inherent in the process of expressing something that is profoundly difficult to articulate.

Two quotes have been essential motivators for this book. The first is from Judith Herman, who wrote "remembering and telling the truth about terrible events are prerequisites both for the restoration of the social order and for the healing of individual victims."[3] Though the women who participated in the project had varied responses to the label "victim," the quote highlights the significance of what they have done. The second is from Brené Brown's talk on "the power of vulnerability" at the TEDx Houston conference in 2010: "maybe stories are just data with a soul." The soul of the data presented in this book are the voices of the women who shared their stories of struggle and resilience.

Acknowledgments

Sometimes we met in the oddest of places—exam rooms in the health center, study rooms in the basement of the library, counseling rooms in the "advocacy center"—but every single time you amazed and inspired me. You *are* this book and though I can't thank you directly by name, you know who you are. Thank you. Sometimes on the way to our meetings and almost always afterward I would listen to this song from the musical *Ragtime* and reflect on your courage:

> Go out and tell our story.
> Let it echo far and wide.
> Make them hear you.
> Make them hear you.
>
> How justice was our battle
> And how justice was denied.
> Make them hear you.
> Make them hear you.
>
> .   .   .   .
> Your sword can be a sermon
> Or the power of the pen.
> Teach every child to raise [her] voice
> And then, my [people] then
> Will justice be demanded
> by ten million righteous [wo] men.
> Make them hear you.[1]

To the women who shared stories in this project—this book is for you.

This project was supported in part by a fellowship from the American Association of University Women (AAUW), which allowed me to focus for a year on interviews and analysis. Since 1881 the AAUW has worked to empower women, and in backing this project they have yet again taken a stand for women's rights.

I am indebted to Greg Britton and Mary Lou Kenney at Johns Hopkins University Press for all of their effort on this book. Greg is a thoughtful and patient editor who challenged me to "explain up" my ideas, and Mary Lou's thoroughness and attention to detail were essential contributions.

Brian Pusser and Nancy Deutsch have been advisors, supporters, role models, champions, and, most importantly, teachers. Their faith in this project made it a reality. Brian and Nancy instilled in me the idea that scholarship can *be* advocacy. Their guidance and training were crucial in this process. Over the course of nearly ten years, Brian engaged me in conversations about "how it could be" rather than reminding me about "how it is," and pushed me to think harder and more critically. He read every draft of this book and offered guidance all along the way. Nancy has made listening into an art form. She taught me to truly and actively listen and observe. While training me in the skills necessary to do qualitative research, she also imparted her passion for informed activism. I could not have had better teachers than Brian and Nancy and their kindness and mentorship are gifts beyond measure. Additionally, Carol Ann Spreen and Diane Whaley provided important insights on this project, helping refine the ideas and find my voice.

Friends and colleagues, especially Whitney Hadley, Angie Henneberger, Caitlin Kelly, Jaime Luce, Jill Martiniuk, and Kayla Richmond, read drafts, introduced me to the wonders of coffee, and were essential to the project. I am grateful to and for them.

My family has provided a solid foundation prior to and throughout this process: thank you for your patience and encouragement. My parents were my first teachers and raised me with an ethic of care and responsibility that led me to pursue this work. They then fortified me as I grew by caring for me in ways that echo profoundly and I am so thankful. To Greg, who has never wavered in his support and who has *lived* the project alongside me, I am incredibly lucky to have found you and grateful only begins to express how deeply I appreciate you. To my son, you have been with me through every step of this project. I was pregnant with you when I spoke with these courageous women and you don't even know yet how you have impacted the way that I think and my level of empathy, but you have. To all of my family, I hope you know that every minute that I spent writing was a minute dedicated to the idea that someday our children and others may be educated in spaces where respect and care are norms.

Finally, I was blessed to know, love, and learn from my grandmothers and my great-grandmother. These women shaped the way I look at the world. Nana Margaret Germain (who always liked to see her name in print) taught me to value hard work paired with a good, loud dose of laughter when things look bleak. Mimi, the grammar police, showed me the impact that a good book can have. And C. Jean Terry, who I carry with the J. initial in my name, gently challenged her grandchildren to find injustice and work against it.

Campus Sexual Assault

1

What We Don't Know about

Campus Sexual Assault

"I don't think anybody fully heard the story."

"Two, four, six, eight, no more violence, no more rape," shouted students at California State University San Marcos. Across the country, at the University of North Carolina at Greensboro, students marched through campus chanting "one in four, no more." Hundreds of students stood on the quad at Brown University in protest of what they felt was complacency among university administrators with regard to the rape allegations of their peers. A pamphlet entitled, "Friends Raping Friends: Could It Happen to You?" was published for college students.[1]

The *New York Times* published articles entitled "Reporting Rape and Wishing She Hadn't: How One College Handled a Sexual Assault Complaint" and "Increasing Rapes on Campus Spur Colleges to Fight Back." The *Boston Globe* ran articles with headlines reading "Lawsuits New Weapon against Campus Rape" and "To Prevent Sexual Assault, Appeal to Peer Pressure." Likewise, the *Washington Post* published "Campus Rapes Create Alarm at College Park" and "How Colleges Vary in Reports of Sex Assault and Other Sex Offenses."[2]

Throughout 2014, students and advocates raised significant public awareness about the alarming rates of sexual violence on college and university campuses. In response, the White House Task Force to Protect Students from Sexual Assault held twenty-seven "listening sessions" with stakeholder groups. In April 2014, the task force released a report entitled *Not Alone* in which they called for prevalence studies, prevention efforts, and changes in institutional and federal responses. The U.S. Senate Subcommittee on Financial and Contracting Oversight also issued a report about how colleges and universities respond to sexual violence. The federal government's emphasis on listening and bringing the issue of campus sexual violence to the forefront should be applauded: campus sexual assault is prevalent, institutional responses have not been effective, and campus cultures are fraught with dangerous social norms related to sexual violence.[3]

Recently, I was teaching a graduate course on the history of higher education in the United States when a student noted that this is the first time the issue of campus sexual violence has received national attention. Unfortunately, this is not true. Although today's traditionally aged college students are likely too young to remember (many were not yet born), half of the articles referenced above were published in the late 1980s and the other half were published in 2014. And while the demonstrations at CSU San Marcos and UNC Greensboro occurred in 2014, the Brown University demonstration was held in 1990, and Jean O'Gorman Hughes and Bernice R. (Bunny) Sandler published *"Friends" Raping Friends*, in which they noted the under-reported nature of sexual assaults, in April of 1987. This is all to say that the issue is not new. Rather, the nation is *again* poised to act in significant ways at the federal, state, local, and institutional levels, and it is critical that these actions be deliberate and well informed.

Campus sexual assault is a pervasive problem within the system of American higher education. If we wish to fully confront the issue, we must examine the many parts of the system as well as the relationships between these parts. The aim of this book is to share the results of a project that focused on a part of this system that has not been widely discussed in academic literature: how college women respond to incidents of campus sexual violence. Rather than concentrate exclusively on themes around hardship and hopelessness, which *are* present in many of the narratives, the book illustrates how women exercised their agency following attacks. I define agency as an equation based on the work of Laura Ahearn: "the socioculturally mediated capacity to act"+intention+action. By concentrating on agency and privileging survivor voices while protecting their identities, my hope is to contribute to the creation of a safer and more supportive higher education system where campus sexual violence is not a norm.

The Prevalence of Sexual Crime against Student Bodies

Deborah Stone wrote that "one common way to define a policy problem is to measure it" and that these "measures imply a need for action, because we do not measure things except when we want to change them or change our behavior in response to them." Accordingly, the prevalence of campus sexual violence has been measured for decades.[4]

In 1957, sociologists Clifford Kirkpatrick and Eugene Kanin published the article, "Male Sex Aggression on a University Campus." They were "prompted by some case material reporting instances of violent male aggression with reluctance on the part of the offended girls to invoke protection and punishment."* The team surveyed 291 women on one campus and found that they had experienced over a thousand "offensive episodes." Kirkpatrick and Kanin's study was groundbreaking in that it introduced the idea of "attempted intercourse and attempted intercourse with violence" within dating or courting relationships on a college campus. As such, although they did not use the phrase "acquaintance rape," the construct was being studied and quantified in the 1950s. Kirkpatrick and Kanin also addressed the emotional responses of women to such unwanted advances and gave language to the range of responses, namely anger, guilt, fear, and disgust.[5]

In the 1980s, Mary P. Koss and her colleagues administered the Sexual Experiences Survey (SES) to thousands of university students in the Midwest (N=3,862) and found that 13 percent of female students had experienced sexual victimization and 4.6 percent of male students admitted to perpetrating acts that would be legally defined as rape. In 1987, Koss along with Christine A. Gidycz and Nadine Wisniewski published the results of a national survey of over six thousand college students from thirty-two colleges and universities in the United States. They found that 27.5 percent of college women reported experiencing rape or attempted rape since the age of fourteen. The study also revealed that very few of the incidents were reported through the criminal justice system and thus would not likely have been reflected in the FBI's Uniform Crime Reports. Furthermore, the study found that prevalence rates "did not vary extensively from large to small schools, across types of institutions, or among urban areas, medium-sized cities, and rural areas." Thus, as early as the late 1980s, the prevalence of campus sexual violence was measured as were the widespread and under-reported nature of such crimes.[6]

---

* The use of the term "girls" is a reflection on the gender mores of the time period in which the study was conducted.

In 2000, with funding from the National Institute of Justice (NIJ) and the Bureau of Justice Statistics, Bonnie S. Fisher, Francis T. Cullen, and Michael G. Turner published *The Sexual Victimization of College Women*, reporting the findings of their research with a random sample of 4,446 women enrolled at two- or four-year colleges throughout the United States during the fall of 1996. Their research approach included two phases and combined behaviorally specific questions, phrased graphically to limit ambiguity, with detailed follow-up. The authors concluded:

> The data suggest that nearly 5 percent (4.9 percent) of college women are victimized in any given calendar year. Over the course of a college career—which now lasts an average of 5 years—the percentage of completed or attempted rape victimization among women in higher educational institutions might climb to between one-fifth and one-quarter. (p. 10)

Additionally, the authors concluded that "an important challenge remains: taking the information found and developing programs and policies that may reduce female students' risk of victimization." This charge remains relevant today and drives the writing of this book.[7]

Between 2005 and 2007, Christopher P. Krebs, Christine H. Lindquist, Tara D. Warner, Bonnie S. Fisher, and Sandra L. Martin conducted the Campus Sexual Assault (CSA) Study. In total, 6,800 undergraduate students at two large public universities were surveyed and 19 percent, or nearly one-fifth, of the female participants reported having experienced attempted or completed sexual assault since entering college.[8]

This small sample of prevalence studies conducted over the last five and a half decades reveals that campus sexual violence is, and has remained, widespread. The first suggestion in the White House Task Force's *Not Alone* report is for more prevalence studies and, while they certainly may help individual campuses to quantify the scope of the issue locally, research from over twenty-five years ago has shown us that the issue is endemic and not limited to certain institutional types or regions. Furthermore, in a competitive culture that is as rankings-obsessed as the field of American higher education, such studies may be problematic if they focus more on the number of crimes than on the culture of the institutions that may make them rape-prone.

Campus Rape Cultures

Campus cultures play important roles in perpetuating dangerous mores. As each new academic year begins, "pop-up" poster sales appear on sidewalks and in parking lots around many campuses so that students and their families can conveniently shop for art to adorn the walls of their residence halls and apartments. The stacks of posters almost always include the iconic image of John Belushi wearing his COLLEGE shirt and drinking Jack Daniels directly from the bottle in the film *Animal House*, despite the fact that today's traditionally aged college students were not alive when the award-winning film was released in 1978. In one scene in the film that has become a classic depiction of American college life, a young woman is passed out in the bedroom of a fraternity member, Larry, and his conscience battles over whether or not to rape her:

> *Larry's evil conscience*: Fuck her. Fuck her brains out. Suck her tits, squeeze her buns. You know she wants it.
>
> *Larry's good conscience*: For shame! Lawrence, I'm surprised at you!
>
> *Larry's evil conscience*: Aw, don't listen to that jack-off. Look at those gazongas. You'll never get a better chance.
>
> *Larry's good conscience*: If you lay one finger on that poor, sweet, helpless girl, you'll despise yourself forever . . . I'm proud of you, Lawrence.
>
> *Larry's evil conscience*: You homo.

By 1979 *Animal House* had grossed over $141 million domestically and it continues to reinforce dangerous and heteronormative ideas about masculinity, sexual coercion, and violence in the ivory tower.[9]

Just one year before the release of *Animal House*, Nona J. Barnett and Hubert S. Feild published "Sex Differences in University Students' Attitudes towards Rape" in the *Journal of College Student Personnel*. In the article, they examined the acceptance of rape myths among male and female college students and found that males were more likely to support dangerous myths that include the idea that one cannot be raped by a person one knows, that "rape only occurs when someone has a weapon," and that "'nice' women don't get raped," among others. Acceptance of rape myths has been linked to victim-blaming attitudes, restricted definitions of rape, and sexist attitudes against women. A 1987 study found that 79 percent of a sample of college men thought that raping a woman was justifiable if the woman was perceived as being "loose." In her groundbreaking 1994 work,

I Never Called It Rape, Robin Warshaw wrote that "because of these myths, the reality of acquaintance rape is largely ignored."[10]

While the specifics of rape myths have varied a bit over time and continue to vary from context to context, two scales have been developed to measure their acceptance. The Attitudes toward Rape Incidents scale and the Rape Attitude and Perception scale have been used to measure the prevalence of myth acceptance and other perceptions or beliefs that can serve as aids in defining rape myths. Rape myths, according to the scales, include items like the ones listed in the previous paragraph. In a 2007 study, the number of sexual partners that a woman had had since entering college was significantly associated with physically forced sexual assault, which may be an indication that rape myths do also impact behavior among perpetrators.[11]

Rape Scripts

A 2009 study published in the journal *Sex Roles* examined the rape scripts of 109 college women. Participants were asked to describe, in detail, their idea of a "typical rape" and to "include information about what happens before, during, and after a typical rape, the thoughts and feelings of individuals involved, and the characteristics of individuals involved." Three common rape scripts were identified among participants' responses and 30 percent or more of the sample described each type of script: (1) violent stranger rape; (2) drug- or alcohol-facilitated rape; (3) date rape. Furthermore, in 78 percent of the participants' descriptions, the outcome of the rape was that the victim was psychologically damaged. Such rape scripts have been coupled in the literature with victim blaming and rape myth acceptance.[12] For example, Sharon Marcus wrote that:

> To speak of a rape script implies a narrative of rape, a series of steps and signals whose typical initial moments we can learn to recognize and whose final outcome we can learn to stave off. . . . The narrative element of a script leaves room and makes time for revision.[13]

This position places the culpability for rape with the individual who has been transgressed upon. The concept of a rape script (or various rape scripts) has been verified within the college student population and is thus worth mentioning. It is particularly noteworthy because on many campuses, including the one attended by the women interviewed for this project, college students themselves participate in adjudication panel hearings including voting on the outcomes of the cases brought forward.[14] If they subscribe to rape scripts that place responsibility with the victims of the crimes, even partially or implicitly, this could impact the questions they ask and ultimately the judgments they make.

The 2009 study of college women's rape scripts also focuses attention on a significant part of conversations about culture and campus sexual assault, namely the script of "drug- or alcohol-facilitated rape" and the social construction of alcohol use and its relationship with campus sexual assault. Several studies have found links between alcohol use and sexual assault among college students. Popular culture is also teeming with prominent images of these links from *Animal House* to the Undercover Colors nail polish developed by students at North Carolina State University. The nail polish allows the person wearing it to detect substances that might have been added to a beverage. By dipping a polished fingernail into a drink, the user can immediately see whether the polish reacts—indicating the possible presence of drugs including rohypnol, Xanax, and GHB that have been linked to incapacitation.[15]

The debate around the Undercover Colors nail polish and whose responsibility it is to prevent campus sexual violence (the people who have to dip their fingers into their drinks or those who put the drugs into the drinks in the first place) also reveals the tension between agency and responsibility when alcohol is involved in cases of sexual assault. Although many studies have linked campus sexual violence to substance use, such findings may also be misleading because they can contribute to victim blaming and the re-enforcement of rape myths. Another study by Hinch and Thomas found that victim blame, sex-role expectations, misinformation, and relationship skills may be related to a person's potential to subscribe to rape-supportive attitudes.[16]

The move from a set of individuals who endorse rape-supportive attitudes to rape-prone cultures is a matter of degree and context. According to anthropologist Peggy Reeves Sanday, a rape-prone society is "one in which the incidence of rape is reported by observers to be high, or rape is excused as a ceremonial expression of masculinity, or rape is an act by which men are allowed to punish or threaten women." Based on prevalence statistics and the number of public rape allegations in the media, the first part of the definition (prevalence) is true for many campuses throughout the United States. Sanday also defines rape-free societies not necessarily by the absence of rape, but as societies wherein sexual aggression is "socially disapproved and punished severely." Looking at media coverage, severe punishment does not appear to be a norm. For example, consider the *New York Times*' coverage of the Tallahassee police department's lack of investigation into a Florida State University student's rape allegations against one of the school's star football players. However, confidentiality is paramount in cases of sexual violence and, as such, we may never learn of punishments for specific cases. That said, perceptions about justice systems are important to think about. Statistics show us that the cultures on many campuses are characterized by violence. We need to strive to better understand campuses and work from both within them and through federal policies to change them. The stories in this book are a starting point for examining campus cultures from an insider point of view and the risk of those cultures on shaping college women's agency.[17]

History of Federal Interventions

In the opening pages of the *Not Alone* report, there is a quote from President Barack Obama from a speech he made in January 2014 when signing the Presidential Memorandum establishing the White House Task Force to Protect Students from Sexual Assault:

> Sexual violence is more than just a crime against individuals. It threatens our families, it threatens our communities; ultimately, it threatens the entire country. It tears apart the fabric of our communities. And that's why we're here today—because we have the power to do something about it as a government, as a nation. We have the capacity to stop sexual assault, support those who have survived it, and bring perpetrators to justice.[18]

In order to think about new solutions to the problem of campus sexual violence, it is useful to look at previous federal interventions and the progress that has been made to date.[19] Title IX, the Clery Act, and the Campus SaVE Act are three important pieces of legislation that have shaped this terrain.

Title IX

"I'm not interested in Title IX, because I'm not a big fan of sports," said a brilliant friend of mine a few years ago. After begrudgingly attending a lecture on the impact of Title IX, it turns out that she *is* a fan of having educational opportunities equal to those of her male peers and of not being sexually harassed in her research lab, among other things. She has since become a mentor for several young women interested in science and gives talks about gender in STEM fields. But, in that moment, she expressed a sentiment about Title IX that reflects both the significance of the legislation for women in sport (which is hugely important) and how little of the impact of the broad nondiscrimination legislation has been discussed in popular media.[20]

Title IX was part of the Education Amendments passed in 1972 and is a federal law that prohibits sex discrimination in all educational programs or activities that receive federal funding. The vast majority of colleges and universities in the United States, public and private, have students attending who receive some level of federal funding, so the law applies to nearly every institution. Discrimination on the basis of sex includes sexual harassment, sexual assault, rape, and other action that "bars the victim's access to an educational opportunity or benefit." The Department of Education receives Title IX complaints and, as of April 2015, there were over one hundred colleges and universities under investigation for their handling of sexual assault cases.[21]

Clery Act

The federal Crime Awareness and Campus Security Act, now known as the Clery Act, is another piece of legislation that relates to campus sexual assault and other crimes. An analysis of the context in which the Clery Act was passed reveals that that moment in American history, the early 1990s, was very similar to the current one in terms of heightened public awareness of campus sexual violence. In February of 1986, Nadine Brozan wrote in a *New York Times* article that "only now is the cloak of secrecy around group rape in collegiate settings beginning to lift," describing rapes at a fraternity party at San Diego State University and three University of Minnesota basketball players who were on trial for the rapes of college women after a game. In the article, Brozan cited the Association of American Colleges project report "Campus Gang Rape: Party Games?" written by Julie K. Ehrhart and Bunny Sandler.[22]

In 1989, the *Boston Globe* ran an article by Anthony Flint with the headline "Lawsuits New Weapon against Campus Rape," in which the story of the 1987 rape of Kristen Buxton by three students at a Colgate University fraternity house served as the opening vignette. The article addressed university investigations and how difficult they can be. Though the men who attacked Kristen Buxton confessed, all received plea bargains and none served jail time. Eventually, Buxton received an out-of-court settlement based on civil charges filed against Colgate and the fraternity. The article serves as an example of the discussions regarding institutional liability and rape that were occurring at the time. In the article, Flint wrote that rape is the "no. 1 form of violent crime at the nation's colleges." He also noted that two other universities, Syracuse University and the University of New Hampshire, were also engaged in investigations into rapes and attempted sexual assaults. Buxton's attorney said that her suit was a way "to force institutions like Colgate to better address campus safety."[23]

In fact, the article cited two cases in which students were successful in their liability suits. In 1987, a student at Miami Dade Community College in Florida was awarded $3 million after arguing that the college's security was "insufficient" to prevent her from being gang-raped in a parking lot. Further, in 1983, the Supreme Judicial Court of Massachusetts ruled that at Pine Manor College in Chestnut Hill, Massachusetts, security was "a contributing factor in the rape of a student." This verdict established that colleges must warn students of known dangers, provide them with "adequate security against foreseeable crime," and be open to charges of negligence, which set the precedent for Buxton's suit against Colgate.

Flint's article also outlined strategies implemented by colleges and universities aimed at reducing rape and protecting students: Brown University's escort service and Harvard's distribution of rape whistles were touted as exemplars. American university officials were seeking instant fixes, band-aids for a larger social problem. Unfortunately, these measures did little to protect students against date and acquaintance rape.

It was during this period that Jeanne Ann Clery, a freshman at Lehigh University, was tortured, raped, sodomized, and murdered in her residence hall. The perpetrator of the crime was another Lehigh student, but a stranger to Clery. He was subsequently sentenced to death. The tragedy of Clery's 1986 assault and murder drew national attention and became a symbol for the movement to reform campus rape laws. In 1990, Jeanne's picture appeared in "The Glamour Report: Campus Rape" and in newspapers across the nation. Her parents became advocates, asking the federal government to act on the issue. The way in which Clery's legacy became a galvanizing factor in political discourse represents what policy analysts call a "horror story" that became an "organizing tool, because it can make a problem concrete, allow people to identify with someone else, and mobilize anger." And mobilize they did.[24]

By the late 1980s the American public was calling for a change. Media attention, academic articles, and student and family demonstrations culminated in concern and fear about campus safety among citizens of the United States. As was the case with Title IX, the public pressed the federal government to intervene. State legislatures had tried to address the matter, but the scope of the issue was so vast that it had captured the attention of the nation.* In conjunction with state policies, grassroots lobbying efforts by students, families (including the Clerys), and other stakeholders put pressure on congressional representatives. Campus crime was subsequently pushed to the top of the congressional agenda. In 1990, President George H. W. Bush signed into law the Crime Awareness and Campus Security Act found in Title II of the Student Right to Know and Campus Security Act. The Act was amended three times and in 1998 was renamed in honor of Jeanne Ann Clery.[25]

Over the years, the Clery Act has changed and expanded in accordance with new information and concerns among the American public. The original Act required all colleges and universities to report institution-level statistics on campus FBI Crime Index Offenses, which include eight specific forms of offense, including burglary, forcible rape, and murder. It mandated the provision of reports on crime statistics to current students, faculty, and staff and the availability of such reports to potential incoming students. It also "encouraged" but did not mandate the creation and implementation of policies to address sexual assault. A primary emphasis of the Act when it was passed was protection through information dispersion. Two years later, the Act was amended to include clauses about the creation of sexual assault policies and their dissemination.[26]

In 1998, President Bill Clinton signed into law the expansion of the Act. The expanded Clery Act increased institutional responsibility to include parts of off-campus areas and required that campus security departments maintain daily logs.

---

* In 1988, the Pennsylvania state legislature passed the nation's first campus-security reporting law. In the following year, sixteen other states passed laws relating to campus safety and crime statistics reporting.

The Clery Act represented a significant bipartisan effort to show the American people that the federal government was "doing something" about campus crime.* Although bill authors changed for each subsequent amendment, the bills themselves received a great deal of support in terms of co-sponsorship and publicity. While the decision-making power rested in the Senate and House of Representatives and the presidents had ratification authority, the key players in each policy debate were not elected officials but advocates like the parents of Jeanne Ann Clery, Bunny Sandler, student protestors, and the media. These individuals and groups united with scholars who provided them with applicable data and evidence from studies and applied pressure on their representatives. In many ways, the process by which the social problem of rape on college campuses was identified and publicized, and the manner in which the American people asserted their interests, was a demonstration of the ways in which advocacy can function as a mechanism for constructive change in the United States.

The Campus SaVE (Sexual Violence Elimination) Act was an amendment to the Clery Act passed in 2013 and signed into law by President Barack Obama. The Campus SaVE Act increases transparency by requiring colleges and universities to collect and report statistics for additional crimes, including domestic violence, dating violence, and stalking. It also requires institutions to further articulate their policies on sexual violence and provide prevention and awareness programming.

One primary goal of the federal legislation thus far has been to increase awareness among stakeholders in American colleges and universities, allowing them to make more informed decisions about which institutions to attend, how to protect themselves, and where to seek help if they experience campus sexual violence. Unfortunately, research suggests that several of these policy goals have not been fully met. In 2001, Steven M. Janosik surveyed 795 American college students and found that less than 4 percent had "used crime statistics in her or his decisions about college choice" and over three-quarters reported not having received (or not remembering having received) an annual crime summary report from their institution.

---

* Congressional representatives identifying with both the political left and right backed the bill from its initial stages and seated presidents representing both parties signed the bills into laws.

Administrators, too, seem to be struggling with how to address campus crimes, particularly sexual assault, and how to interpret the Clery Act and its implications.[27]

The *Not Alone* report by the White House Task Force to Protect Students from Sexual Assault is the most recent step in the process of working toward substantive change. After prevalence studies and prevention work, the third recommendation in the report is to "help schools respond effectively when a student is assaulted." In order to work toward this goal, it is imperative that we continue listening.[28]

If schools are to "respond effectively when a student is assaulted," their efforts must be informed by the behaviors and perceptions of students who have experienced campus sexual violence. A great deal of the research literature on campus sexual violence examines its prevalence (something that we know has, unfortunately, remained pretty consistent over time) and the institutional support and reporting mechanisms that many students do not use or have negative experiences with. However, in a 2003 study, close to 90 percent of women who survived completed or attempted sexual assault reported that they had disclosed the crime to a friend.[29] Further, many women have come forward through public and social media to raise awareness about the ways their institutions have handled cases of sexual assault over the past several decades. So, students who have experienced sexual violence on campus *are* (and have been) talking about their experiences, but many existing institutional policies and structures do not seem to have been built based on the information that has been bravely shared. Unfortunately, this lack of listening has led to a disconnect between policy intent and policy effectiveness: reporting rates continue to be low and barriers to support-seeking within institutions remain.

The Project

Driven by the need to better understand the issue, I began collecting stories from college students who had experienced sexual violence while enrolled at a mid-sized university on the East Coast. By interviewing students, I could provide a safe forum for expression because their stories could be de-identified, combined, and shared in aggregate. The goal was to inform institutional responses to campus sexual violence by learning how women exercised agency following attacks at the University. The purpose of the project was to work with students who had experienced campus sexual violence, to explore their post-assault experiences and perceptions in hopes of informing institutional responses so that they take into account what people *actually* do following experiences with campus sexual violence. The goal was to examine the forms of agency that women exercised and to begin creating processes and policies that are supportive of their decisions and instincts in context.

I chose to focus on students who self-identified as female not because the stories of male-identified students or students who identify as transgendered are any less important to hear. Statistics suggest, however, that female-identified students are a primary risk group for campus sexual violence, and I had to somehow bound the potential population. I strongly suggest that additional studies be done with male-identified and transgendered populations as institutions create and enhance policies and support systems.

The first step in the process was to speak with representatives from the groups that provide resources and support services on campus and in the community around the University in order to become familiar with the services that were available to students. Many of the resource providers gave me referral materials to share with participants after interviews if they wanted them. I also met with a representative from the University's sexual violence adjudication board to learn about their processes and procedures. Staff and faculty from several different departments and centers on campus allowed me to schedule private rooms in which to hold interviews so that women could choose convenient spaces where they felt secure. Representatives from many of these groups asked for reports or ideas about how they could improve their services based on the study.

Next, the interview protocol was constructed and refined. It was then piloted with two women who identified themselves as having experienced sexual assault as students, but who were not members of the University's undergraduate student body at the time of the interview. Based on their advice, the protocol was finalized. The final protocol was designed to be used flexibly and to solicit narratives about women's experiences and perceptions prior to and following instances of campus sexual assault and rape. I was careful not to use the terms sexual assault, rape, victimization, victim, or survivor unless asking specific questions about the labels, because I wanted the women to tell their stories in their own ways using their own words and definitions. Instead, I intended to mirror the terminology they used within the context of our conversations.

The next step was something of a leap of faith. I put up flyers around campus. I emailed the individuals in control of the student list-servs at each of the colleges within the University and asked if they would include information about the project in the weekly or monthly emails sent to students. Every college sent out the message to all of their students, so every undergraduate student enrolled at the University received a notice in her or his inbox.

The flyers and emails that were sent out shared the institution's sexual assault prevalence rate. They also shared some of the details of the project and asked students who were willing to be confidentially interviewed to contact me via a secure email address. The flyers and emails closed with a quote from Judith Herman, "Through them, we realized the power of speaking the unspeakable and witnessed firsthand the creative energy that is released when barriers are lifted."[30]

"Do you really think that college students will come talk about their experiences to a stranger in an interview?" People asked me some variation of this question for months as I talked about starting up the project. "Don't you think the sample will be biased because only some people will come forward?" they would often continue. My answers were: (1) I think that they *will* come talk to me if they know that the project is about informing institutional policy makers about how students actually respond to attacks, and (2) Yes, I do think the sample will be biased, but it will include more people than policy makers at the University have heard from so far.

Within days of the first email being sent out, I began receiving responses. After the first few interviews, participants told their peers about the project and more came forward once they knew that the project was legitimate and safe.

By the end of the fall 2011 semester, we had more concrete answers to the questions posed above: (1) twenty-eight students came forward to participate in the project within the ten weeks of interviews (twenty-six of them were undergraduates), and (2) the sample is certainly biased toward individuals willing to come forward and talk to a stranger, but at the same time, the stories of more than two-thirds of the women had never been heard by a representative of the campus administration. (For more information on participant demographics, case details, and methodological notes, see appendixes A and B.)

Interviews

Individuals responded to the call for participants by sending an email to an address created for the project. They were then sent in-depth materials about the project and a consent form to read. If they chose to participate, they were asked where and when they would like to meet. I also asked if they felt comfortable having me interview them and informed them that if they preferred another interviewer, there were other options. I am thankful to have had two colleagues, one of whom is male-identified, volunteer to facilitate interviews using the protocol for the project in order to offer options to potential participants. The majority of undergraduate women who emailed about the project elected to participate in interviews (26/28) and all interviewed with me.

I would then reserve the room of the woman's choosing at the time of her choosing and tell her how to recognize me. At the time, I was carrying a rather large, colorful bag full of resources, protocols, and a recorder that made me easily identifiable. I met each woman and we talked about the project for a few minutes. Once they said that they felt comfortable, we began the interview. Each session was audio-recorded and ranged in length from 45 to 153 minutes, not including preliminary conversations and questions about the project, demographic questions, or negotiations about follow-up, etc.

I owe a great debt to the work of Ann Oakley and Marianne Paget who argued for and described a "science of subjectivity" that can be established through interviews. It was important to me that the project be focused on listening actively and including the women to the fullest extent possible in an effort to privilege their statuses as agents and owners of their stories. As I subscribe to Oakley's philosophy about interview subjectivity, I think that neutrality in an interview between people with aligned purposes is not necessary for the legitimacy of the project. I don't believe that distanced subjectivity is the pinnacle for all interview-based work. Rather, in this case, I think that even the perception of such "objectivity" could have been perceived as deceitful and perhaps even counter-productive: there was no point, in my mind, in pretending that my goal was anything other than to collect stories and bring them together in an effort to strengthen the campus community through a better understanding of women's responses to campus violence. I have been trained in and have conducted many interviews from the distanced-observer standpoint, but that approach did not fit this project. For these reasons, and because I believe that the women being interviewed were incredibly important, I do not refer to interviews as being *conducted*, but rather as being *facilitated*. I approached each interview as a "search-process" in which the woman telling her story and I worked together to seek meanings in context. Together, in the interview spaces, we would work toward an understanding of the woman's story and her perceptions.[31]

The Web-Forum

Melanie Millar defined cyberfeminism as "a woman-centered perspective that advocates women's use of new information and communications technologies of empowerment."[32] Blending notions of campus communities, collaboration, connection, reflexivity, and cyberfeminism, I created a private, secure web-forum for the women in the project. At the end of each interview, I explained the forum's goals of connecting the women in the project to one another, to me, and to the project as it progressed. I gave each woman log-in information and explained that she could either sign on using her own email address or, if she chose, we could create an email address that would veil their name from the rest of the participants. With one exception, the women elected to use their own names and email addresses if they used the forum.

The web-forum virtually connected women who wanted to share with one another throughout the process of the project. I could also post questions about the project as they arose. One particularly poignant moment occurred in an interview when a woman said that she was feeling "totally alone" because none of her friends had experienced (or at least had told her they had experienced) anything like what she had. When she signed onto the forum, she became part of a community of women who had experienced campus sexual violence and, if nothing else, she could see that she was not alone. Another woman spoke with me about how she had been considering writing a letter to the person who attacked her and asked me to post a question on her behalf asking the other women in the web-community for their insights. Within twenty-four hours, a woman who had written a letter to a student who attacked her responded with her thoughts.

Participants shared lists of Bible verses and other resources that were helpful in their healing. As such, the site may have contributed to a sense of collective agency among participants.

The web-forum was also a space for accountability and transparency about project themes. For example, when the preliminary findings were written up, I uploaded them to the web-forum and asked for feedback. Two women emailed me directly with their feedback and agreed that the findings represented their views.

Stories as Analytic Vignettes

Throughout this book, I use analytic vignettes labeled "stories" to illustrate themes from the project. The way I use these stories is nontraditional. Analytic vignettes can be important evidence that helps honor the voices of participants. According to Angela Creese, in her analysis of linguistic anthropologist Nancy Hornberger's work, vignette use can bring to light "complex, detailed, illustrative and realistic accounts of research participants" revealing "variability, nuance and detail."[33] As such, I wanted to include analytic vignettes from interviews in this text.

However, there is a significant challenge to using women's narratives directly: in the context of interviews, many women shared important specifics about their experiences and identities. Some of these details, particularly when combined, could be used to identify women. For example, women named the residence halls they lived in, talked about social organizations they belonged to and jobs they held, stated friends' names, and noted whether or not they had pressed charges. Protecting the identities of the women with whom I spoke was important, but so too were the details of their stories, so I decided to use a hybrid aggregate vignette model where a blend of two or more narratives is used to obscure the identity of each woman. No elements in the vignettes have been fabricated, but components and quotes from more than one interview illustrating the same theme are incorporated together for identity protection.

My Assumptions

Like researchers Marjorie DeVault and Glenda Gross and others, I viewed this project as being constructed *for* and *with*, rather than merely *about*, women and their experiences. DeVault and Gross argued that active listening is critical to the creation of knowledge that is *for* participants.

Because this was a collaborative project, many measures were taken to honor the women's stories. First and foremost, I accepted what the women told me and valued their words. These women came forward to talk confidentially with a stranger for an hour or more about being attacked in hopes of making the system better for others. There was no benefit to them other than perhaps a sense that they were part of a collective action project. Research also supports the likelihood that women were telling the truth; a 2010 study by Lisak and colleagues found the percentage of false allegations "reported to a major Northeastern university over a 10-year period" was 5.9 percent.[34] It is, then, conceivable that a couple of women were not telling the truth and I'm willing to accept that possibility.

Another significant assumption that I brought to the project is that there is no optimal post-assault set of behaviors, feelings, or perceptions. As such, the primary question in interviews was, "please tell me about the experience that led you to volunteer for this project" and, from there, the interview progressed according to what she shared.

The women made many choices throughout the project: they decided when and where the interviews should take place and whether to use their real names on the web-forum or to use the forum at all. Women were also given the opportunity to provide feedback on the project's findings. Further, the interview process gave all of the women the chance to define and label the elements of their experiences and identity themselves. Participants were also asked to comment on potentially problematic language devices such as sexual assault and assailant ownership terms (for example, "her assault" and "her perpetrator").

Finally, I know that the sample for the project is likely not representative of all female college students who have experienced campus sexual violence. I spoke with women who were willing to come forward and talk to a stranger about their experiences. However, while a sample that does not fully represent the whole is a significant limitation of the project, it would have been nearly impossible to engage in a project of this nature with a random sample of the population of individuals who have experienced campus sexual violence.

So, is this project classist, sexist, and does it reinforce gender binaries? Yes, unfortunately, all of the above are true. The site is a university and, as such, it is both a privileged and a privileging space. Sexual violence is not limited to college campuses. However, the site represents many college and university spaces where the rates of sexual violence are incredibly high. Additionally, while the University and colleges and universities in general are privileged spaces, they are also spaces in American society with substantial, planned acculturation rituals (campus tours, orientation sessions, branding, residence life trainings, convocations, etc.), recognized leadership, and policy. They are spaces that are, in many ways, simultaneously autonomous and governed by state and federal governments. They are accountable to many stakeholders: students, faculty and staff, investors, states, the federal government, and the public at large. So, while the project does focus on a privileged space, the space can be viewed as a microcosm for society at large. Moreover, policies developed to prevent sexual violence, and to "respond effectively" to sexual violence in the meantime, can start within these institutions and grow to impact society as a whole.

In terms of sexism and the reinforcing of gender binaries, as I said before, unfortunately at this moment in history the prevalence statistics suggest that female-identified students are most at risk. In no way do I think that the narratives of male or trans-identified individuals are unimportant, they are simply not in the bounds of this project: they need attention in both literature and policy. Further, all of the women who participated in the project were assaulted by males and research has shown that most perpetrators are male.[35] This does not mean that assaults where the perpetrator is female or trans-identified are unimportant; it means that none of the women with whom I spoke described assailants as female or trans-identified. All of this said, it is always important to consider the voices that are not being heard. In this case, that is the voices of male and trans-identified people as well as the voices of women who did not participate in the project.

What Can We Learn from the Project?

Although the project may not be representative of the experiences of all students who have faced campus sexual violence, it is no less informative. Among the narratives of the twenty-six undergraduate women who participated in the project there was great heterogeneity. There were also many similar themes that need to be recognized and added to conversations about both prevention and support for those who experience sexual violence. While there is a body of literature outlining what many women do *not* do following experiences of campus sexual violence (for example, how rarely college women press charges), little attention has been paid to what women actually *do* and why. Yet, the theme of post-assault agency ran throughout all of the narratives, and the ways that women exercised their agency in incredibly challenging circumstances deserves recognition.

A lack of research that positions the voices of students who have experienced campus sexual violence at the center has left federal, state, and institutional policies and structures informed by prevalence statistics and assumptions. Research has revealed that students disclose incidents of campus sexual violence to peers. Consequently, there has been a call for the implementation of bystander intervention programs: an important and significant contribution to prevention and survivor support work. It is important to note, however, the many ways that students who have experienced campus sexual violence act as agents themselves: deciding what resources to utilize or not utilize; deciding whom to tell and not tell; acting to protect themselves; acting to achieve justice outside the bounds of the institutional or judicial systems; and others.

Post-Assault Agency Forms

In total, there were eight forms of post-assault agency exercised by the women in the project:

- Embodied Agency—corporeal actions: actions in preservation of, service to, or using the body (for example, cleansing the body)
- Managing Identity—acting in attempt to control the way in which one is perceived (for example, cutting one's hair in an attempt to appear less attractive)
- Silence—choosing not to share one's story with one or more people or institutions
- Self-Expression—outward assertion of one's thoughts, feelings, or story (for example, through the creation of artwork)
- Pursuit of Individually Defined Justice—working outside of existing structures to attain a personal sense of justice or closure (for example, writing a letter to educate a perpetrator about the impact of his actions)
- Transitive (Formal)—working in conjunction with an institutional system, most commonly the college or hospital (for example, pressing charges with an internal university adjudication board)

- Transitive (Informal)—working in conjunction with another individual or group toward a purpose or outcome (for example, asking a friend to walk one home)
- Empowerment—independent or collective actions that demonstrate or amplify social, political, or spiritual power (for example, leading a Bible study for women who have experienced campus sexual assault)

Because there is overlap in the eight forms of post-assault agency in the narratives, the book has five chapters into which the agency forms are classified and illustrated. While women's stories and their exercise of various forms of agency were diverse, a narrative arc emerged that was shared by many, so the book is organized to reflect that general pattern. Chapter 2 addresses embodied agency and describes how most women showered or slept in the immediate aftermath of attacks. Chapter 3 is about managing identity. Decisions about identity tended to begin after leaving a situation or upon waking up after an assault and continue from there. Chapter 4 focuses on disclosure and silence and outlines women's decisions about whom to tell and whom not to tell. Chapter 5 is about justice, both as institutionally and legally defined, and as women themselves defined and sought it. Chapter 6 focuses on women's empowerment, something that for most women happened months, if not years, after being attacked. There are lessons for policy makers, campus officials, faculty members, families, and friends in their stories about finding their way after campus sexual assault. The book's concluding chapter discusses the ways that shifting to an agency framework and listening to the stories of students who have experienced campus sexual assault can impact policies and support services.

2

The Paradox of Embodied Agency

"Apparently that was the wrong thing to do."

How do we understand the issue of campus sexual assault? On college websites and in campus rape prevention materials, students are told not to walk alone at night, to avoid certain places, to walk in well-lit areas near blue safety lights that can be used to call campus security officials, and to "watch what is going on around you"—along with a plethora of other strategies for basic crime prevention. Taken at face value, the advice is not bad. There are dangers associated with walking alone in the dark, not paying attention to your surroundings, and being intoxicated. But the great majority of college students already know these things. What's more, most of the prevention strategies listed, while valuable overall, are based on misunderstandings about campus sexual assault. Furthermore, such prevention strategies set expectations for the manner in which many college women believe they will be treated following experiences of campus sexual violence: namely, the expectation that if they did not behave in the manner outlined in prevention emails or according to the established post-assault protocols, they do not deserve (and will not receive) institutional support or justice. Examining real cases of campus sexual violence as described by women who endured them illustrates some of these misperceptions and leads to a more nuanced and representative way of understanding campus sexual assault and college women's responses to such transgressions. In turn, we can begin to re-conceptualize prevention and support strategies in a manner that is more informed and sensitive to the needs of college students.

Alice's Story

Alice and Zack attended the same high school and had known one another for several years before they both began attending the University.

The two were in different majors and colleges within the institution, so they didn't see one another often, but Alice considered Zack a friend.

One evening, as Alice was walking home after hanging out with friends at a local restaurant and bar, she saw Zack. He was alone, stumbling and struggling to walk. He was holding onto a bench trying to stabilize himself. Alice became worried and decided to help her friend get home safely. When she later reflected on the situation, Alice shared that she did not feel threatened by the circumstances since she and Zack had been friends for many years and Alice herself was sober. Furthermore, Alice explained, she had a boyfriend and Zack had a girlfriend, so she did not perceive any danger.

Alice took Zack by the arm and helped guide him back to his room on campus. When they arrived, she poured him a glass of water in hopes that it would help him to "sober up" and possibly avoid being hung over the following day for class. Alice was surprised when Zack asked her to lie down next to him. At first she hesitated, saying that she felt "weird" about the request. But then Zack responded by saying, "oh whoa, you know, like, I have a girlfriend and you have a boyfriend—this doesn't mean anything." So, Alice decided to humor Zack and lay down to talk to him for a bit.

As Alice lay talking casually with Zack in an effort to ensure he was safe so she could excuse herself from his room, he grabbed her, held her down, and got on top of her. He began to sexually assault her, forcibly removing some of her clothing. Alice tried to push him off, but due to the angle and his weight, she was unsuccessful.

Next, Alice tried to reason with Zack. She told him that she didn't like what he was doing, she asked him to get off of her, she told him that he would regret it in the morning, she mentioned his girlfriend. None of these efforts stopped Zack.

Suddenly and seemingly out of nowhere, Zack smiled and asked Alice if she was "comfortable." She replied by saying that she wasn't. Laughing, Zack said, "I don't want this to be rape" as he continued to hold Alice down with his body weight and hands. Alice responded, "Well, it will be because this is not okay."

As Zack continued to assault Alice, she tried another approach: distraction. She asked Zack to use a condom, and he agreed. When he stood up to find a condom in his cluttered bedroom, Alice used the moment to get out of the bed and find her clothing so that she could leave. As she rushed to put her clothes back on and escape the situation, Zack asked her if he could walk her home, explaining that she would then not have to walk alone at night and be in danger. Alice told Zack that she preferred to walk home alone and ran from the room.

When recounting the event months later, Alice shared that she was still very confused about Zack's response. In asking if he could walk her home, Zack sounded to her like "someone who is being thoughtful and considerate of [my] well-being, but he had just done this horrible thing." ■

Alice's experience represents several major challenges to the "don't walk alone at night" strategy of campus sexual assault prevention. Zack's invitation to walk Alice home in order to keep her safe from harm reflects the notion that the threat to students is external to the campus community.* Yet, Alice's story shows that a major threat to college students dwells within the campus community itself. While external threats do exist and warrant recognition, decades of sexual assault prevalence research has shown that most college students are assaulted by acquaintances. In fact, in twenty-four of the twenty-eight cases described in this study, the perpetrator was a peer the student knew and had no reason to distrust. Moreover, from the moment the students at the University had stepped on campus for orientation, they were taught to trust one another and the campus community, which may lead to a false sense of security among peers.[1]

Furthermore, a primary assumption of such "prevention" strategies is that campus sexual assault can be avoided by showing confidence, not walking alone at night, and not drinking. Although these behaviors may be effective anti-crime strategies in general, they perpetuate a system of victim blaming because many crimes cannot be prevented by these means alone. Additionally, such strategies for prevention set up a "perfect victim" icon against which college women and others can compare true stories and decisions.

The "Perfect Victim" Icon

The perfect victim icon is made up of a collection of media images and campus crime prevention messages. You've seen "Her" in news stories and you've read about how "She" behaves in emails from campus

* Zack's offer to walk Alice home also reveals a common assumption that only female students are in danger; Zack would presumably have to walk home alone after Alice entered her residence hall.

administrators. She is a successful and social student. She was not drinking the night that she was attacked by a stranger. She explicitly said "no"
and she fought back. The attack left her bloodied and bruised. She went to
the emergency room "to seek medical treatment IMMEDIATELY" and did
not bathe, brush her teeth or hair, change her clothes, or go to the bathroom so as not to destroy evidence as per the university's recommenda-
tions. She told the police her story right away and there was not a single
variant. She was scared, but totally rational throughout. She was upset,
but not hysterical.[2]

When I spoke with real college women who had experienced campus
sexual assault, they often made reference to the perfect victim without
naming her as such. In many cases and in different ways, women compared
their own experiences and choices to hers in an effort to determine if they
had done the "right things" and would be taken seriously. In this way, the
perfect victim is problematic: She sets an unrealistic standard that individuals who experience campus sexual assault, and those interacting with
them (whether they are peers, parents, administrators, adjudication panel
members, or others), use as a metric to gauge and judge survivor behavior.
In essence, she is a large part of why victim blaming and systemic revictimization occur. In being so highly publicized, she shifts the focus of
the problem from the perpetrator to the survivor. Her very presence, particularly her starring role in prevention campaigns, signals the idea that
the survivor who does not look or act just like her is the root of the problem. In order to shift the focus of prevention from the survivors to the
perpetrators, we need a more nuanced, realistic understanding of what
women actually do following experiences of campus sexual assault.

The narratives of Alice and her peers illustrate many of the forms of
agency that college women use in the time following these experiences.
In telling their stories, they shift the paradigm from prescriptive and
idealistic to descriptive and truthful. The operative question that can
drive changes in the way we think about campus sexual assault then becomes "what did women actually do in the minutes and hours after being
attacked?"

The answers are different for each woman. Yet, there are significant
elements that unite the narratives. The first of these features is that
women acted to preserve and protect their bodies during the attacks and
immediately afterward. In the example provided by Alice's story, the ini-

tial forms of agency were survival and escape. Escaping from the immediate threat or context was the first form of post-assault agency exercised by
many women in the study.

Alice tried to push Zack off of her, in doing so she exercised agency
through physical force in an attempt to escape the attack. Other women
reacted with similar displays of physical force. For example, one woman
who experienced attempted sexual assault while outside at a party shared
the following:

> There was a railing around the porch so I'm just grabbing onto the
> railing and he was pulling this way around (gestures to indicate direc-
> tion) so I'm still here and I think one of my elbows gets loose and I hit
> him—like trying to get him off somehow—I don't get him very hard but
> I think it like startled him enough that like he let go and I got back inside
> the house . . .

Although in some cases women were able to hurt or surprise the perpetrator enough to stun them and escape, many women, like Alice, were
not able to escape by using physical force owing to the constraints of
the situations.

The notion of physical force itself is problematic. First, in most cases,
women were unable to use force to stop the attacks because of the size and
power differentials between them and their attackers. Some women were
stunned, incapacitated, or immobilized by fear. In reflecting on these experiences, women made comments like, "it's not like I hit him or anything."
Their comments reflect their own comparisons of themselves to the perfect victim, who fights back. Second, some women compared their injuries
to those that they had seen on the perfect victim, whether on television or
on the news ("it's not like I had bruises"). Again, the perfect victim icon set
up a false reality about what "counts" as force, and therefore what "counts"
as sexual assault. Incongruence between their own experiences and those
of the perfect victim were connected with questions about whether or not
they deserved justice.

After her attempt to physically fight off Zack, Alice attempted to reason with him. She told him that she was uncomfortable and that what he
was doing was "not okay." She reminded him about his girlfriend, and she
told him that he would later regret what he had done. In her attempts to
reason with Zack and use intellectual force to escape, Alice was not alone.

Several women talked about employing such strategies, although in most cases they were unsuccessful.

Resisting by shouting or screaming was another strategy the women employed. In one case, a woman was raped outdoors while a social event happened inside. The event had loud music that made her screams impossible for others to hear. Other women did not scream for various reasons that ranged from shock, to embarrassment, to fear of escalation. Yet *not screaming* was another way that women found fault with their own behaviors when compared to those of the perfect victim. Several women worried that the people to whom they told their stories would not believe them because they had not screamed to stop the attack, and thus, might be perceived as having consented.

Most of the women in the study either used physical force or intellectual force in attempts to escape situations of campus sexual assault; some women tried both. In some cases, peer intervention was an additional critical mechanism for enabling women to escape attacks. Bettina's story focuses on the important connections between survival and peer-enabled escape.

Bettina's Story

Bettina and Will had been friendly from the time that they moved into the same residence hall. They often saw one another in the mailroom and hallways. Bettina recalled that sometimes the two even flirted. One day, Will was on Bettina's floor of the building and stopped by for a brief visit. As he left her room, he jokingly swiped one of her books and ran down the hallway with it, yelling to her to come get it back from him. Will ran into the stairway and up to his room with the book.

Before Will's visit, Bettina had been getting ready to meet some friends for dinner. When they arrived minutes after Will ran away, she told them that she would catch up with them in the dining hall and went to retrieve her book. She needed to get it back, even if it meant being late for dinner, because she had an exam the next day and needed the book for studying.

When Bettina got to Will's room, the two began flirting in a way that Bettina believed to be harmless. As Bettina tried to grab her book and run away, Will laughed and held onto it. Bettina enjoyed flirting with her neighbor. She was having fun until Will stood between her and the door and locked it so she could not leave.

Next, he sprang at her and pinned her down on his bed. At that moment, the situation changed for the worse. Will held Bettina down, picked up a t-shirt off of the floor and forced it into her mouth so that she could not breathe or shout. He began to forcibly remove her clothing as she struggled to breathe. Bettina later described being "paralyzed with fear" and repeating to herself, "it'll be over soon, it'll be over soon."

After several long moments, Bettina still isn't sure quite how long, the doorknob began to jiggle from the outside as Will's roommate tried to open the door. Will yelled for his roommate to leave and, when the jiggling stopped, he took the t-shirt out of Bettina's mouth, put his thumb on her windpipe, and pushed down so that she was gasping for air. Bettina continued to tell herself "it'll be over soon, it'll be over soon" as she struggled to survive. When Will heard his roommate at the door again, he finally stopped, and Bettina was able to grab her clothing and escape from the room.

Days later and without yet speaking about the incident for fear of being humiliated, Bettina sent her friends to collect the book that Will had taken from her. ■

Peers, like Will's roommate, were often crucial to women's escape and survival. Perhaps, without even knowing it, Will's roommate assisted in Bettina's eventual getaway.

As with escape through physical or intellectual force, survival through mechanisms like Bettina's internal refrain, "it'll be over soon, it'll be over soon" are another aspect of embodied agency. There are three other primary ways that women exercised embodied agency or took actions to protect and preserve their bodies in the immediate post-sexual assault context: cleansing, resting, and collecting evidence.

Cleansing and Sleeping

Almost every woman discussed the importance of cleansing her body at some point in her narrative. Women sharing their stories with me used words like "grimy" and "dirty" to describe the way they felt following attacks. Many women spoke about taking showers upon returning home as they tried to manage the physical and emotional sensations. Several women spoke about water temperature extremes such as "freezing" and "scalding" in their attempts to cleanse their bodies. For example, one woman described her thoughts in the hours following an attack:

I'm so disgusting, oh my god. So, I just like sat in the shower for about twenty minutes. Scalding hot water, and I was just like, oh my god, oh my god, like I kept praying that I would just wake up and it would've been the worst nightmare in the world.

Showering and cleansing were also used in women's long-term coping and healing work. For some women, showering was a way to manage recurring negative feelings or flashbacks. One woman, in talking about coping strategies, recommended journaling and showering sequentially, she said:

I definitely like to journal and then a lot of times after I journal, I like to take a shower. It's just, all of a sudden, you're in the shower, you feel clean and you feel refreshed: it doesn't matter if you were like super angry about something . . . all of a sudden, it kind of all just is better.

Many women in the project spoke about nightmares. Some experienced nightmares they could vividly recall upon waking and others had nightmares that left them with feelings of anxiety and fear upon waking, but no clear memory of the dreams themselves. When asked how she coped with nightmares, one woman explained that showering was beneficial. She described waking up with "a cold sweat on" and said that she would then "often *have* to go shower" to make herself feel better, though she would still find herself unable to sleep.

Claire's Story

Claire awoke in a pile of blankets and pillows on the thin carpet that covered part of the tile floor of her bedroom. After being sexually assaulted by a peer with the same major and with whom she took many of her classes, Claire just needed to sleep.

During the attack, Claire urinated in her bed. Once the assailant left the room, she did not have the energy to clean her bed sheets as she was exhausted and stressed. So, she threw her pillows and a clean blanket down onto the floor beside the bed and fell asleep there. Claire continued to sleep on the floor beside her bed for several nights because she needed the rest and she did not want to "deal with" the urine on her bedding. Days later, Claire used a search engine to privately look for ways to clean her mattress and then engaged in an extensive cleansing process. ■

Claire was not alone in her need to sleep following an experience of campus sexual assault. In fact, after showering, sleeping or attempting to sleep was the second most frequent form of agency employed by college women in the hours following these experiences. The most common reason women provided for sleeping (or trying to sleep) was an effort to seek privacy and comfort. Beds and bedrooms were some of the only non-shared spaces available to these women, most of whom lived communally with other students in either residence halls or apartments. Other women spoke about going to sleep as a way to attempt to gain a sense of normalcy or to compartmentalize what had just happened. One woman said, "I went to sleep and I was kind of trying to act like it didn't happen"; another said, "I just, I think I just really have a tendency to like, cognitively compartmentalize all the emotional crap in my life. And it's just like a little box, and like, I'm gonna deal with you later, shut up. Go to sleep, right now." Further, as most assaults occurred at night, going to sleep was the "normal" thing to do. Unfortunately, many of the same strategies that women used to survive during and following being assaulted put them in direct conflict with the perfect victim icon and, therefore, posed challenges to their seeking help or justice through formal mechanisms.

The Paradox of Embodied Agency

Students have been instructed by the University to follow a specific protocol after an experience of campus sexual assault. They are advised to seek immediate medical treatment and not to bathe or change clothes. Yet, the majority of women who shared their stories in this project either showered or slept first, and many did both. While these actions may seem like "natural responses" to sexual assault, they are exercises of agency because they are actions motivated by physical and emotional needs and mediated by the culture of the campus that tells students *not* to do them. Only one woman I talked with went immediately to the emergency room after the assault, and two others went there after sleeping for several hours. None of the women reported going to the University's website looking for tips on how to handle experiences of CSA immediately after being assaulted (although some did web searches later).

The desire or need to cleanse one's body immediately following an experience of sexual violence is not uncommon. Scenes of women standing in showers have been depicted in film and television to indicate that sexual violence has occurred. In her book *Watching Rape*, Sarah Projansky notes that "the post-rape washing scene becomes a trope, a very brief moment outside the narrative flow that stands in for 'women's experiences of rape.'" So the act of cleansing can be powerfully representational as well as a practical act not only for individuals who have experienced sexual violence, but also for the consumers of media from rape-supportive cultures. Yet, showering is framed as the "wrong" thing to do because it eliminates DNA evidence.[3]

Just as showering removes DNA and other trace evidence from one's body (for better or worse), increased time elapsed between the sexual assault and a post-assault physical examination reduces the likelihood that signs of injury will be found by an examiner. One study showed that within twenty-four hours of an assault, there was an 89 percent likelihood that physical injuries would be detected. This chance was reduced to 46 percent after seventy-two or more hours. This is why women are encouraged to seek emergent care as soon as possible. Yet an important and commonly described post-CSA behavior was sleeping or trying to sleep. Further, some women talked about sleeping but did not frame it as a choice. "I just like crawled into bed," is one example of this, as is falling asleep owing to impairment or incapacitation.[4]

In the immediate aftermath of experiences of campus sexual violence it was often the case that some actions critical for proper evidence collection were not aligned with what women themselves were seeking. Often the idea of evidence-collection and case-building came second to a woman's need for self-care. Thus, I spoke to women who felt that they needed to shower or sleep in the immediate aftermath of attacks and only later really focused attention on justice-seeking. Other women thought about justice-seeking immediately, but decided to prioritize private self-care.

The perfect victim would not make such calculations or decisions. She would follow the directions given by the University regardless of her own needs or desires. Thus, as each woman compared her actions to those of the perfect victim, she expressed feelings of guilt and self-blame over decisions to shower and rest following incidents of campus sexual violence. For example, one woman said, "I just, like, I wanted to take a shower and apparently that was the wrong thing to do if I wanted to get a rape kit." The notion that a rape kit, or the set of tests that are performed in a medical setting following a sexual assault in order to obtain evidence from the body of the victimized person, was necessary in order to effectively press charges was commonly held among the women in the project. Many women believed that formal justice would no longer be attainable if they cleansed their bodies, slept, or did anything other than immediately go to the emergency room because they felt that it would limit their credibility due to the lack of physical evidence available to them. Yet, most women elected to shower and sleep anyway. Thus, the paradox of embodied agency is that women want or need to cleanse and rest their bodies following attacks despite the belief that doing so may reduce their ability to seek justice later. Quite literally, many women described watching their chances of pressing charges go down the drain as they fulfilled their primary needs to be safe, clean, and rested.

In fact, twenty-two of the twenty-six women I met with for this project decided not to press charges through the school or anywhere else. A principal reason many of the women elected not to press charges was the lack of physical evidence to substantiate their cases. Women perceived the lack of physical evidence to be a reason they would not be believed if the case were brought to trial or a board hearing. One woman summed up these sentiments by saying, "One of the main reasons I didn't report it was because I had no physical evidence whatsoever. So, I felt like I wouldn't be taken seriously." Another woman shared a similar perception, stating that she would not press charges "because it's a he said / she said type case. There were no witnesses; there was no physical evidence. He is probably going to deny it if ever asked . . . it's, I feel like, the University would have a lot of problems accepting just my story." It was clear that many women didn't have confidence their testimony would be believed without physical evidence or a witness, which made their decisions for self-care in the immediate aftermath indeed seem paradoxical to them. Their decisions to care for themselves first moved them further from the perfect victim and, in their understanding, further from the justice system.

Elusive Justice

The women in the project described two potential avenues for the pursuit of formally defined justice: the institution's adjudication process or the legal system outside of the University. Just two women referenced engaging with the legal system outside of the University: one had obtained a restraining order from the local municipality and another was in the process of deciding whether or not to press charges in civil court following a finding of "not responsible" from the institution's panel. The more common avenue for the pursuit of formal justice was through the University and involved pressing charges that would be heard and decided upon by a panel of students and faculty.

Women's perceptions of the institution's adjudication processes significantly impacted their decisions about whether or not to pursue justice at the institutional level. These perceptions were summed up with this statement from a woman in the project, "I just hear about how they haven't expelled anyone in, in like thirty years." The results of panel hearings are confidential, so there is no public record of whether or not anyone has been punished. Yet a commonly held belief among women in the project was that the University simply does not punish students for perpetrating sexual assault. Peer networks were important in perpetuating this perception:

> I know people who did [press charges through the institution] and nothing happened . . . like I guess I should have tried myself, but . . . there are still a lot of people who were like, "yeah, that doesn't work, my friend tried that and the person doesn't get kicked out."

Another woman shared that her friends had told her that "very small amounts [of sexual assault] are prosecuted and even smaller convicted" at the school. The belief that the expulsion and suspension rates were either minuscule or nonexistent was often cited as a reason not to press charges. Despite these perceptions, four women did elect to press charges. In three of these cases, women had gone to the emergency room within twenty-four hours of being assaulted.

Diana's Story

Diana was raped by a fellow student at the University. After being attacked in the middle of the night, she passed out for several hours. When she woke up, she was incredibly disoriented and had a horrible headache despite having had only a small amount to drink. Diana had a difficult time making sense of her surroundings and, after speaking with a few friends who she had been out with, Diana began to believe that she had been drugged. It was the only thing that made sense considering how she felt, what had happened, and how little alcohol she had consumed.

Though Diana desperately wanted to shower, her friend "basically dragged" her to the emergency room. Once there, Diana decided that she would do everything "by the book" in hopes of convicting the perpetrator using the school's system. After waiting several hours at the emergency room and speaking to the police, Diana was offered a rape kit and elected to have it administered. The tests confirmed that sexual intercourse had taken place. However, neither the kit nor the police investigators' interviews could confirm that consent was withheld. The assailant later claimed that Diana was intoxicated but gave consent. In Diana's opinion, the investigator did not "do a very thorough investigation" and she felt that he treated her "more like the suspect." Additionally, Diana believed that the investigator was mis-informed about the perpetrator. She said the investigator "was looking for some sort of hoodlum, you know, or someone else like a bad guy. And, like, [the perpetrator] was very suave . . . He's a student . . . he doesn't look like a bad guy."

Diana's case was brought before the school's sexual assault adjudica-tion panel. Despite the physical evidence, in Diana's opinion it was a "he said/she said" case because the evidence could only prove that sexual in-tercourse and injury had occurred, not that it had not been consensual. Diana characterized the perpetrator as more charismatic and a better pub-lic speaker than she was, and she was incredibly embarrassed and upset while giving her testimony, which she believed shaped how the panel per-ceived her. At the hearing, a member of the adjudication panel asked Diana why she had waited so long to go to the hospital if she was really raped. Diana's case resulted in a not responsible finding.

In reflecting on her experiences, Diana said:

It was the only way I could really find, like, comfort in all this, I was like, I'm just kind of going to do everything by the book 'cause what else can I do? . . . So I'm just gonna do everything that seems to be the right thing to do. So, yes, I'll go to counseling even though, I don't think I'm counsel-able. [Chuckles] I am apparently [counsel-able]. Like, okay, yeah, I'm go-ing to tell the police this happened. I'm going to press charges with the school and now I'm going to press charges civilly because *the school doesn't care* . . . that's the only way I feel like, I can at least find some clo-sure, even if he's not guilty civilly either, at least I tried. I just, I can't like live with a little secret like that . . . I, I like to fix things. ■

Diana's story illuminates several themes common to the narratives of the women who elected to pursue justice through the University's system: there is a "correct" or "by-the-book" way for a woman who has experienced campus sexual assault to behave; a woman should go to an emergency room and have a rape kit administered; filing a formal complaint affords an opportunity for some "closure"; and "the school doesn't care."

Diana's opinion that "the school doesn't care" was born of her experiences with administrators and those associated with formal adjudication proceedings. Like many colleges, the University has an adjudication board comprised of students and staff/faculty trained to work on such proceedings and maintain confidentiality. Diana was not alone in personifying and vilifying "the school." Many of the women in the project spoke about "the administration" or "the school" in abstract but negative terms. However, it is important to note that *individuals* working within the administration or as representatives of the school (such as counselors, student health professionals, etc.) were often specifically cited for their positive efforts. That is, on the whole, one person could make a difference for a student, and students could name the individuals within the administration or the school who impacted their process (both for better and for worse).

Embedded in Diana's story is a narrative about evidence collection and rape myth acceptance. In all of the cases where women sought hearings through the University, physical evidence was a factor. Diana and another woman believed that having had rape kits administered at the emergency room, along with telling their stories to detectives and SANE nurses (sexual assault nurse examiners), their cases would surely meet the burden of proof necessary to find the assailants responsible. In the other case, the women recognized that the lack of physical evidence was a major shortcoming.

The woman who decided to press charges through the institution's panel without physical evidence echoed the sentiments of those who elected not to press charges saying, "there's no evidence and, like, the defense attorney could turn it around to say it was consensual because it's, like, his word against mine, so . . . there's no case really." Yet, what made her case and the case of a fourth woman who was in the process of pressing charges against a perpetrator enrolled at another college different from cases where women without evidence chose not to press charges were their perceptions of institutional support. In both cases, the women reached out to administrators about the incidents. Neither woman was immediately seeking to press charges, but both were exploring options related to their academic trajectories in the aftermath of violence. They were seeking guidance about things like deadline extensions or moving out of classes in which the perpetrators were enrolled. In both cases, leading administrators supported them and encouraged them to file charges. Without this encouragement, the woman had felt there was no case to be made. Thus, the efforts to acquire "proof" through a trip to the emergency room and the administration of a rape kit or to garner legitimacy through consultation with an official at the institution were linked to decisions to press charges through the institution.

The Perfect Victim on Trial

Another common theme among the cases that went to hearings was the role of rape myths and the perfect victim icon. In two of the cases brought forward to the University's student adjudication board, the women were assaulted by strangers (although the strangers were fellow students). Diana's perception that the police investigator was looking for a "bad guy" rather than a student reinforces the normative dichotomy between assailant/bad guy and student/good guy. This is aligned with the findings in previous help-seeking studies which have shown that women are more likely to press charges against a stranger than an acquaintance. It also aligns with the myth that stranger rape is more common than acquaintance rape, which evidence has refuted. Another way the perfect victim icon emerged in hearings can be viewed in the question to Diana about why she waited several hours before seeking medical attention.[5]

The final common thread between the cases brought to hearings was that whether or not physical evidence was collected, none of the three cases heard at the University ended in a finding of responsible. Although the physical evidence obtained through a rape kit could confirm contact, it could not prove consent, and campus sexual assault cases at the University require one to prove that consent was not present. In response, one woman said that her case and others like hers were "worthless."

Yet, even with evidence, the cases are still perceived as "he said/she said" events. So, the perception that "very small amounts [of sexual assault] are prosecuted and even smaller convicted" at the University stems from the belief that little can be done. In the two cases where students felt they had support from administrators, one had not yet gone to hearing at the time of the interview and the other ended in a finding of not responsible. Another woman, who was a former student employee of the University, suggested that she would never tell an administrator about what happened to her because she doesn't think that they have the power to "*do* anything.*"

The narratives of twenty-six college women who have experienced CSA incidents tell us that there is no single correct path, or set of goals, or needs that applies to every person and situation, and that a considerable set of challenges awaits. The perfect victim icon is held up as an unreasonable standard for all survivors against which they and others measure the efficacy of their actions. Furthermore, others use the perfect victim image to judge women's decisions in a manner that perpetuates blaming of the victims and a lack of understanding in the culture. Yet embodied agency matters. It was employed by Bettina to survive the crime, it enabled Alice to seek escape, and it offered cleansing and rest for Claire. For others, embodied agency in the aftermath of campus sexual assault included going to the emergency room to seek medical treatment and for the collection of evidence. And yet employing some forms of agency can be transgressive of powerful norms of behavior and these women had to make essential decisions about their own needs, often with insufficient support, in a very short, complicated, post-trauma window.

   Our culture constructs women's bodies in such a problematic way that the measures that women take to protect and preserve themselves following violent transgressions are called into question and, in many cases, are antithetical to the established processes for seeking justice. In 1998, psychologist Nicola Gavey wrote that "within a rape trial the constant scrutiny has been on the woman and her body; it was she and her body that must be interrogated in order to see whether she invited that trouble—the rape—on herself." Unfortunately, over a decade later, the prominence of the perfect victim icon on college and university campuses perpetuates such scrutiny to the point where women like Alice, Bettina, Claire, Diana, and their peers are left weighing self-care against the pursuit of justice.[6]

3

Managing Identity

"I didn't want to be the bad girl."

Eva's Story

Eva was in bed with her eyes closed, but she was awake. She silently debated whether or not she was at fault. She thought, "I could have freaked out, I guess, I could have made it into a public scene, and I would have solved things . . . mostly," meaning that if she had screamed while being raped, she *might* have been able to alert nearby students who *might* have intervened, perhaps her yelling *might* have stopped the attacker. ". . . but I didn't, because I didn't want to be a bad girl, and so I let myself get into a situation that I wasn't comfortable with."

After a lot of thought during many sleepless nights like this one, Eva eventually decided not to press charges against the perpetrator (through either the legal system or the University's sexual assault adjudication board). She made the decision not to press charges because she did not believe that her account would be trusted: after all, she thought, she could have made a "public scene" by yelling or going immediately to the emergency room following the assault. She had been frozen with fear during the attack and had made almost no sound. Afterward, she went home and showered for a very long time.

Based on her actions during and following the assault, Eva thought that she would not be viewed as innocent. She thought she would be judged as a *bad girl*, which would limit or remove her right to pursue formal justice against the man who raped her.

Rather than have her integrity called into question, Eva did not pursue formal charges and worked to maintain regularity in her life by acting as "normal" as possible and not telling most people what had happened. ∎

Many of the women I spoke with described feelings similar to Eva's: the desire or need to exercise agency to manage the ways that others perceived them in the aftermath of sexual assault. Identity and agency are interconnected when women act or decide *not* to act. It is an exercise of one's agency to think about and act in an effort to preserve, change, or otherwise impact the way one is perceived. Like Eva, most of the women decided not to press charges because they feared their identity and character would be called into question. Their feelings align with the work of psychologist Judith Herman, who wrote that "at the moment of trauma, almost by definition, the individual's point of view counts for nothing . . . The traumatic event thus destroys the belief that one can *be oneself* in relation to others."[1]

It is important to point out that most women who participated in the project did not believe that they couldn't be themselves in relation to *all* others. In fact, lots of women described others, most commonly peers and family members, with whom they felt they could absolutely be themselves. Yet, almost every single woman I spoke with discussed some way in which she did not act authentically in an effort to manage perceptions of herself and either keep things in her life the same or shift them in the aftermath of violence. Through this performance of identity, some women reclaimed a sense of control. In Eva's case, she decided not to press charges and to maintain her typical routine, even if it meant pretending to sleep at her usual bedtime so that her roommate would not note a change. In working to appear as though things in her life were normal and not call attention to the incident, she was able to control perceptions of herself or how she was "read" by others in her environment. She, and many of her peers, did not want experiences of campus sexual violence to define them. Poignantly, one woman explained that if a dean on campus knows of her, she wants it to be because of her accomplishments and not because she was assaulted.

Identity management (that is, managing the ways that people viewed them), took two non–mutually exclusive context-driven forms: diffraction (altering the self) and homeostasis (remaining the same).

Diffraction (Altering Identity)

In physics, diffraction occurs when the path of a wave is altered at the moment it comes into contact with an obstacle. Like waves, some women shifted the ways they performed their identities so that they were perceived differently in the time following attacks (obstacles). In some cases, diffraction was intentional; in other cases, women described feeling as if they were in a fog and not necessarily making deliberate choices. For some women, diffraction meant changing their behaviors; for others, diffraction meant changing their appearance: some women did both.

Fiona's Story

Fiona was raped by a fellow student whom she knew well. She wanted "to crawl under a rock" in the hours following the attack. Ordinarily fastidious about her hygiene, beauty routine, and overall appearance, Fiona explained that the day after being attacked "the idea of getting up and getting dressed and facing the day and doing, like everyday normal things was such a daunting thing" that she did things differently. That morning, she didn't put on her usual make up and she dressed in her "crappiest clothes" in an attempt not to "look good at all" and to "blend in." Over a year later, when we spoke, Fiona had returned to her pre-assault appearance and routine. ∎

Georgia's Story

Georgia, a student-athlete who was assaulted by a member of another athletic team at the University, had long hair at the time of the attack. She also had a muscular frame that helped her excel at her sport. The University, like many with competitive sports, has an athletic complex that includes dining areas, practice spaces, and gyms. Most athletes at the University spend significant time in the sports complex and eat lots of their meals together using the campus meal plans. In this context, Georgia saw the person who assaulted her (and his friends) on a daily basis. She even had to eat her meals in the same room with them. She described feeling nervous when she was near them and, based on some of the comments they had made about her body, she began to believe that her appearance made her a target for their attention. In the weeks that followed the attack, she cut her hair into a cropped "pixie" style and lost approximately ten pounds. She correlated these changes with the diminishing attention she received from the male athletes at meals and in the gyms and said that, "they just, like, leave me alone now." ∎

Both Fiona and Georgia acted (diffracted) in an attempt to avoid the sexualized gazes of their peers by altering their appearances and typical routines. Other students diffracted by skipping classes even though it was out of character for them: one said that she began missing classes when she realized that the student who raped her was in her class. Even though the class was large, she was afraid she would see him. In fact, she "stopped going out as much as possible" during the semester following the attack because she was fearful that their paths would cross. In this way, diffraction also meant changes in the ways that women performed their academic and social identities.

Homeostasis (Maintaining Identity)

The human body maintains its temperature by controlling the creation and release of heat in response to changing conditions. This is an example of homeostasis, which is defined as the "tendency of a system . . . to maintain internal stability, owing to the coordinated response of its parts to any situation or stimulus that would tend to disturb its normal condition or function."[2] Many women I spoke with acted to maintain the perceptions that others held of them despite having experienced campus sexual violence (having their normal condition disturbed): they shared stories about maintaining their usual habits so that no one would suspect that something had happened. Some women described their actions as stemming from confusion/shock, for example, "I didn't know what to do and I was already late to dinner with my friends so I just went and met them." Other women described acting very intentionally: when recounting the morning after she was assaulted, one woman, Hope, declared, "I went to class . . . I'm not gonna let this be who I am." She was not alone, several women said that they did not want their professors or teaching assistants to think they were "slackers" so they went to class, sometimes just hours after experiencing assault. Just as skipping class diffracted academic identities while preserving a sense of safety for some students, attending class despite having recently experienced trauma was a way that other students maintained homeostasis in academic identity.

Work toward maintaining homeostasis, whether intentional or not, was not only undertaken in an effort to manage the perceptions of others. Time and again, women spoke about maintaining their eating, sleeping, and exercise routines in order to also maintain a sense of their pre-attack selves. For example, several women talked about going to the gym or running at their typically scheduled times in the days following attacks. Yet, the perceptions of others were often linked to a sense of preserving one's pre-attack self: all of the women, for instance, related that in at least one instance they had chosen not to share their experience because they did not want it to define them.

Using Silence to Maintain Homeostasis

The concept of silence has been understudied in work on campus sexual violence. Yet silence, as broadly defined, was a significant theme in women's narratives. Silence was most often described as a *decision* invoking both intent and action and therefore can be conceptualized as a form of agency.

Previous studies on post-assault behaviors have focused on the decision not to press charges and remain silent in relation to courts and adjudication panels.[3] In this project, the definition of silence was expanded to include and value all of the things that women did following incidents of sexual assault, not only those that have been used to compare women's choices against perfect victim iconography (for example, reporting to authorities). Silence included, but was not limited to, not telling authorities / pressing charges. It included electing not to tell any person or group of people. With this definition, the most frequently cited and equally relevant reasons that women chose silence were: (1) self-protection; (2) protection of the perpetrator; (3) protection of a social group; and (4) protection of family and friends from the "burden" of knowledge.

Discussions of silence for self-protection often invoked identity maintenance or homeostasis: women did not want perceptions of themselves to change or to be defined by what had happened. Additionally, self-protection was linked to the notion that lack of proof would lead to revictimization before the board. Women feared they would not be believed if they pressed charges. As one woman put it, "one of the main reasons that I didn't report it was because I had no physical evidence whatsoever. So I felt like I wouldn't be taken seriously." Another woman described the process of pressing charges as potentially "horrific."

When women spoke about protection of perpetrators, they often described guarding perpetrator identities and reputations either by not telling people about the incident or by not disclosing their names (for more on disclosure, see chapter 4). However, a few women spoke about protecting perpetrators from physical harm by not telling male peers or boyfriends who they thought might attack the assailants. Social groups that women spoke about protecting through their silence included groups of student workers, Greek communities, athletic teams, and others. Protecting family and friends from the burden of knowledge referred to the desire to shield people they cared about from the pain they felt as a result of having been assaulted. Most frequently, multiple reasons were behind any one decision to remain silent.

Imogene's Story

Imogene enjoyed Greek life at the University. She lived in her sorority house and was very close with many of her sorority sisters. She even met her boyfriend through the Greek system: he was a member of her sorority's long-time "brother" fraternity. The two organizations often hosted formals and parties together. The arrangement between the two groups was very convenient for Imogene and her boyfriend because they were able to spend a lot of time together. That is, until one of her boyfriend's fraternity brothers raped her.

After the assault, Imogene described feeling "numb" for several days as she went about her usual routines in an attempt to not call any attention to herself. Only when she was alone did she allow herself to think about what had happened. She worried about her reputation, her friendships, and her relationship with her boyfriend. She also worried that if she didn't do something about it, another woman would be assaulted. Imogene described herself as "strong" and began to think about pressing charges against the attacker, but she knew it would be challenging.

Nearly a week after the incident, Imogene decided to tell her boyfriend what had happened. She anticipated that he would be angry at his fraternity brother, but supportive of her. First, she asked him not to get angry with her. Then, she told him the whole story and said that she was thinking about pressing charges.

When recalling this disclosure over a year later, Imogene shared that her boyfriend did not respond how she imagined he would. Her primary concern had been that he might try to physically harm the attacker. Instead, he asked her not to press charges and told her that if she did, she would put the entire fraternity at risk. He warned that if Imogene reported the incident, the University would be required to inform the national branch of the fraternity, and he feared that the national branch would respond by putting the entire house on probation. If this happened, her boyfriend fretted, he and many of their friends in the fraternity would not have a place to live the following school year.

Distressed by her boyfriend's response, Imogene turned to a group of her sorority sisters for support. She believed they would understand her concern about the assailant raping another woman, even if he had been a friend. Again, she was surprised by the response she received. She said that some of the women didn't believe her and brushed her off right away. Others were kinder but encouraged her not to report the incident because it would strain the relationship between their sorority and the fraternity.

In the days that followed, Imogene decided not to report the incident and to remain silent about what happened in order to preserve her relationships and reputation and not disrupt her community. She did not speak about what had happened with her boyfriend or most of the women whom she had told.

Later, Imogene regretted her decisions. The more she thought about it, the more she worried about other women. Additionally, she was having a difficult time sleeping and focusing. She realized that her boyfriend's response was not supportive of her at all, and she broke up with him. Eventually, she deactivated from her sorority, remaining friends only with the women who had been supportive both of her and of her decisions. In her interview, she shared that she continues to feel guilty about not pressing charges and still worries that the perpetrator will rape another woman. ■

In an effort to maintain homeostasis and protect herself and others, Imogene decided not to formally report what had happened to her. She disclosed the incident to peers on two occasions and the idea of pressing charges to protect others was not supported either time. In fact, she received the same message from both her boyfriend and her sorority sisters: do not report the assault because it will put both of our social groups at risk. Imogene did not talk about the assault again for months in an effort to preserve her relationships and not be seen as causing trouble for her boyfriend, friends, or the two organizations. After she left the sorority and her boyfriend, she continued to keep what had happened to her a secret from many people in her life. She remained friends with only a few of the sorority sisters who had been supportive of her healing (even if not all of them had endorsed pressing charges) and spent more time with friends outside of the Greek system at the University. Like Hope, Imogene did not want her experience with sexual violence to define her in the eyes of others.

Imogene's story illustrates the importance of the many subcommunities that make up the University's student body. In Imogene's case, the Greek community, particularly the close relationship between her sorority and the fraternity, played a major role in her decision-making and the advice that she was given by peers. Her decision to disclose the incident to her boyfriend and peers revealed her trust in them. Their suggestion that she act to preserve the organizations reveals their desire to maintain the status quo and not disrupt the system despite the act of violence that had occurred within it. Thus, the choice to remain silent by not pressing charges and not speaking of the attack after her two disclosures was linked to maintaining homeostasis for Imogene herself, as well as for her friends, by preserving the norms of their social environment. However, in preserving these norms, Imogene worried that other women would be at risk.

Imogene came forward to participate in the project because she hoped that sharing her story would help shift the culture at the University so that future students wouldn't have to go through what she did. She said that she felt very guilty about not reporting the incident at the time since doing so may have protected other women, but when she finally left the Greek community there was no way for her to press charges as too much time had elapsed and she felt that both her former sorority and the fraternity would work to discredit her.

Subcommunities embedded in the larger University community played many different roles in women's narratives. Some subcommunities of students were supportive of women and their decisions. However, within this project, many of stories that involved *more than one* member of an all-male peer group were negative. As constructs, collegiate male peer groups such as fraternities and athletic teams *do* have a bad public reputation when it comes to campus sexual violence. Too often there are elements of these communities that are misogynistic whether or not the misogyny is obvious or intentional. Yet, these communities are typically comprised of many members and the cultures within them are not homogeneous even on the same campus. Athletic teams and fraternities often hold significant power and privilege on campus, as is the case at the University. Their members can impact the culture of the institution in significant ways for better or worse. If members of these groups subscribe to rape-supportive attitudes and engage in misogynistic and/or violent behaviors, they can significantly impact the rape-prone nature of a campus community. However, if they subscribe to anti-rape and anti-violent attitudes and promote a culture that is supportive and safe for all members, they can impact the nature of the campus community for the better.

Jennifer's Story

It was Jennifer's first visit to the gynecologist, and she was incredibly anxious. She had asked a friend to call the student health services center and make an appointment for her, but she did not explain why. When the doctor asked the reason for her visit, Jennifer said what she had rehearsed: that she was considering having intercourse with her boyfriend whom she had been dating for a long time and wanted a prescription for birth control pills. She told the doctor that she was a virgin, but she was concerned that during the physical exam the doctor would be able to tell that something was different. After the uncomfortable exam, Jennifer went to the drug store and picked up a prescription for birth control pills. Despite having no intention of having intercourse, she continues to take the pills daily.

Jennifer had been assaulted a couple of days before she went to the health services center. In her interview, Jennifer told me that she was a virgin at the time of the assault. She wanted a prescription for birth control pills because she was afraid of being raped again. She did not want to talk with the doctor about being assaulted. She explained, "so I just kind of made up this lie . . . I just wanted to be safe in that situation if anything happened." Jennifer still questions whether she is a virgin or not. ∎

Managing identity sometimes involved cultural and religious group identities. Several women shared that they were virgins before being attacked and more than one discussed whether or not she could call herself a virgin anymore as a result. A few of the women referenced their religious or spiritual identity in relation to their virginity; experiences of sexual violence challenged their faith and sense of self.

Other women included (and in some cases, referenced several times in our conversations) aspects of their identities or roles that implied agent status. Such roles included athlete, member of a military training group, leader of a student organization, and resident assistant. These roles indicate agent status because they involve some degree of power, training, and often membership in an important or influential group. Thus, some women managed their identities both in their lived experiences and in how they described themselves in their narratives.

Using Silence to Protect Others

Jennifer did not tell her parents what had happened to her because she did not want them to be upset and because she worried they would make her leave the University. Like Jennifer, several women spoke about choosing silence in an effort to preserve homeostasis in their familial relationships and close friendships. When women spoke about electing not to tell people what had happened in order to preserve their relationships, the term "burden" was often used. For example, one woman said:

> I feel like one of the things that's hardest for me is I feel like a *burden* on other people when I share my problems . . . I always try to be open and be there for other people, but I always have a problem reciprocating, in a sense. And so that's been like, I think, the hardest part, it'd be opening up to other people.

The notion that telling their stories would force others to bear witness to something that might be difficult for them to hear was a significant motivation for some women not to speak about what had happened. They described the desire to protect those who cared deeply about them from pain. In such important relationships, some women also worried about becoming objects of pity. One woman worried that her mother would be so upset that she would make her leave college if she knew it was not a safe environment.

The reverse was also true. Some women shared that they felt they *had* to tell family members and close friends in order to maintain homeostasis. In these cases, women said that those closest to them seemed to know something was wrong and they felt compelled to share what had happened in order to re-establish normalcy in their relationships (for more on this, see chapter 4). This also illustrates that efforts at identity diffraction and identity maintenance (homeostasis) were not mutually exclusive in narratives. In fact, most often women did both.

Academic Identity

Women talked directly about their grade point averages (GPAs) and expressed concern about the impact of the assaults on their GPAs as metrics of success in college. For example, one woman who went to class only for tests after the assault said, "I just went to class if I had an exam and I did very poorly. I mean obviously [it] totally slammed my GPA." Another woman was raped at the end of the semester and explained that she was unable to concentrate or sleep well while preparing for her final exams and, as a result, her grades for the semester had suffered. She worried that one semester of work that was uncharacteristically low would impact her options in the future by lowering her GPA and raising red flags that employers or graduate programs might inquire about. In the same vein, a woman explained that she would never have pressed charges because it was possible that her name would be leaked and she felt that being associated with a case of sexual assault, even if she were the plaintiff, could negatively impact future employment because people would not want to hire someone who was in any way associated with something like campus sexual assault.

Two students took semesters off; one said, "I told them I do have depression and I do have insomnia and I actually took a semester off junior year." She and her family did not feel that being on campus was healthy for her and she explained that she was lucky that she was able to leave at a point in the semester that allowed her to not have any failing grades recorded on her transcript.

Records of academic success (transcripts) and their connection to future employment were important to many women, but so too was their overall academic reputation. One woman turned in a paper late after being assaulted and missing the class when it was due. Nervous that her professor might think she was not taking the course seriously, she decided to tell the professor what had happened. She did not share the details of the assault and was careful to explain that she did not want an extension on the paper; she simply did not want to be viewed as disrespectful of the faculty member or course.

Revisiting Diana's Story

In chapter 2, we learned about Diana's friend bringing her to the emergency room after a fellow student assaulted her. Diana described her desire to proceed "by the book" in terms of evidence collection and pressing charges. Though the tests confirmed that sexual intercourse had taken place, there was no proof that consent had not been obtained, and it was too late for tests to detect any traces of "date-rape" drugs in her system. When the police investigated the case, Diana said that they seemed to be looking for a "hoodlum" or a "bad guy"; in contrast to such myths about perpetrator identities, Diana characterized the assailant as "very suave" and "a student." This reveals much about the role of perceived perpetrator identity in cases of campus sexual violence. In the same way that women who have experienced campus sexual violence are compared to the perfect victim icon, perpetrators are compared to a standard that is unrealistic and stereotypical. The very notion that the detective might be able to tell if the perpetrator did not "look like a bad guy" implies that there is a construct of what a "bad guy" looks like that can be applied to potential perpetrators. So, the perfect victim icon and the construct of the stereotypical perpetrator intersect to make cases particularly challenging to adjudicate with panels.

When Diana described herself and her testimony to the panel, she self-identified by her major in a STEM* field and characterized herself as naturally reserved. She believes that the perceptions of the panelists of her as a person played a role in their finding of not responsible.

During the hearing, both Diana and the man who attacked her were asked to offer verbal statements to a panel of students and faculty charged with determining whether sexual assault had occurred. Following these statements, the panelists asked each of them questions. Diana described feeling incredibly uncomfortable with the proceedings. Not only did she have to speak about the degrading and painful experience in front of strangers, she had to do so in front of the perpetrator. She then listened to his testimony, in which he argued that she had been drunk but had given consent.†

When talking about the hearing, Diana noted that the perpetrator was an extrovert and incredibly charming to the panel as he gave his testimony. She described herself as a bit awkward. She also said that she was not sur-

---

* Science, Technology, Engineering, and Math

† It is not uncommon for the person pressing charges and the accused individual to be in the trial/proceeding room together.

prised that the panel believed him over her as his testimony was more compelling due to his personality. ∎

Diana's story reflects the way that perceptions about identity intersect with conceptions of justice. The University's published definition of effective consent, which would have applied to her case, included a clause stating that if a student knows that another is drunk or otherwise incapacitated, effective consent cannot be given. During questioning, Diana's attacker said that Diana had been very drunk at the time of sexual intercourse (Diana believes that she was drugged as she did not have much to drink that evening), thus making effective consent as defined in the policy impossible. There was physical evidence that sex had taken place and lack of effective consent, but the assailant was not found responsible by the panel. Is it possible that perceptions of identity played a role in who was and was not believed? Diana herself believed that identity played a role in the decision rendered in the case.

Diana was not alone. Many women in the project suggested that incapacitation or coercion, intimidation or threat (rather than physical violence), were reasons the University's adjudication board might not take their cases seriously. Yet, all of these words were components of the University's definitions of campus sexual violence. However, one of the most significant reasons that women did not to press charges was fear that they would not be trusted in a "he said / she said" case because of how their actions and identities would be perceived. Several women thought their word would not be trusted in hearings or trials because they couldn't prove that "force" was used against them. One woman put it this way: "I said no. I said don't do it, but it's not like I hit him . . . like, I just let it happen. So I don't know how much of a case I would have. Um, you know—*it's not like I have bruises or anything.*" To her, bruises would have been a way to show the physical force used in the attack. Without bruises, she feared, adjudication board members would not believe her; she felt they would think she hadn't fought back hard enough.

Katie, a gender studies major, elected not to press charges because she thought her identity would impact the panelists' perceptions of her:

[The University] is the epitome of patriarchy . . . *They* won't believe me. . . . And if he denied it, like, who are you going to believe? The gender studies major? . . . And at the time, I was going through my radical feminist phase and I didn't shave my legs and stuff. And it's like, are they going to believe me? Like, are they going to think that I'm just being a whiny feminist? You know, and I just—I was too terrified of it . . . knowing that I knew that I was right was much more comforting than, like, putting it up to a vote.

Katie believed that her academic identity as a gender studies major, her social identity as a radical feminist, and her physical identity (including unshaven legs) would work against her in the eyes of the adjudication board.

The University is required by federal law to make its definitions of rape, sexual assault, and effective consent accessible to students and other stakeholders and it does. Still, most of the women who participated in this project did not believe they would be able to successfully press charges because events would be *interpreted* and then defined by panels. Many women felt it unlikely that a panel of peers, faculty, and staff would trust them over a male peer. Several women felt that student defendants were advantaged over them because siding with defendants maintained homeostasis within the campus community and meant that the University would not have to report a sexual assault in its crime statistics. Because hearings on cases of sexual violence at the University are confidential (for the protection of all involved), most students do not know the actual numbers of students found responsible for these crimes. However, the commonly held perception among women in the project was that the adjudication board was decidedly pro status quo and therefore rarely, if ever, found anyone guilty or responsible. It is an exercise of agency to decide not to put her reputation on the line for a process that was unlikely to end in a result that she considers "just."

After experiencing campus sexual assault, identity mattered to women in significant ways. Some sought homeostasis so that no one would know anything had happened to them; they didn't want to be treated differently. Others attempted diffraction by changing themselves physically or shifting their routines in an effort to garner less attention from assailants and other potential attackers. Women were challenged to reconcile their experiences of campus sexual assault with their overall identities. Some wondered if they could still be considered virgins. Many questioned whether or not the label of "victim" applied to them. One shared that she struggled with the application of the word "survivor" to herself because it has so often been used to refer to people who have survived diseases like cancer and she didn't feel her experience fit into the same category. Most women rejected either the term "victim" or "survivor": some rejected both. Many worried about their academic identities and future career identities. To them, perception often was (or felt like) reality, and the way that others responded to them was critically important.

4

Telling Friends and Family

"I just I didn't admit to myself that I was raped, until like . . . like ever . . ."

"Rape" and "sexual assault" have been defined in many contexts. There are legal definitions that vary from state to state, institutional definitions that vary by site, cultural definitions, and others. Legal and institutional definitions are used to delineate the boundaries of crimes and other forms of misconduct. When a person engages the justice system, she or he must somehow express what has been experienced and compare that against a legal or institutional standard.* There is risk associated with the use of the labels "rape" and "sexual assault" because once such labels are applied, one can become subject to the scrutiny, experiences, and identities associated with the victim label. For example, when juries or institutional adjudication boards are involved in proceedings, their cultural understandings of such terminology (including rape myth acceptance) may play a role. However, before applying legal and institutional definitions to their experiences, the women in this project focused on expression that was far more fundamental: they explained how and to whom they first disclosed these experiences.

The verb "say" means "to give expression to" or "to express with words." As simple as this may seem, the act of verbal expression about one's experiences of sexual violence can be exceptionally complex; the act itself involves acknowledgment of what happened, the application of a term or some form of symbol to represent the event, considerations about identity,

---

* This evaluation of wrongdoing does not only happen within the context of trials and hearings; women also compare their experiences against standards and rape myths in deciding whether or not to engage such systems.

and an audience of some type.* Professor Annie G. Rogers wrote about the "unsayable" nature of some forms of trauma. She argued that the unsayable can take "a coded, symbolic form" and "insist" that it somehow be expressed whether through behaviors or words. Women in the project talked about the behaviors and words they first used to express their experiences and who they selected as their audiences.[1]

The Importance of Labels

A central finding of the project is that although there were shared themes among women's narratives, the narratives themselves were heterogeneous. As such, it is not surprising that the use of labels held varying levels of importance for women in the project. For some women, labels were empowering or central to their narratives. Others found labels unimportant or even limiting.

One woman said that she feels that "rape is a more honest word" for what she experienced. She continued, "I feel like rape is just, like you hear the word and everyone in the room just [she cringes physically as she pauses] I don't know, but yeah, I prefer the word rape." When asked if she preferred the rape label because it elicited a stronger reaction from people, she agreed, adding, "because it is personal and awful and the term sexual assault for me, personally, doesn't get at that and from my experience, I was raped." For her, other terms did not fully describe what she had experienced, and she wanted people to know what she had been through.

Other women spoke specifically about electing *not* to use formal labels. One woman described her experience as "a textbook sexual assault" but added, the way those words "sound and feel . . . it's just awful." Because of this, she elects not to use a label but rather describes what happened when she chooses to share her experience with someone. Another woman talked about *trying* "not to label things that happened" because "right now I just want to move on with my life." Though women used labels with different levels of comfort and significance, the desire to describe experiences without using the rape or sexual assault labels was embedded in many narratives. A common theme was that the labels of rape or sexual assault are often difficult to say and for others to hear.

* By audience, I do not necessarily mean a group of people. In this case, I mean a disclosure site of some type: one person or a group.

Laura's Story

Laura was barefoot, shaking, and carrying one shoe as she walked to her building. Her other shoe was still somewhere in his bedroom, but returning to retrieve it was not an option. She had told him, "no." She had tried to fight him off, but he was just too big and she had never physically fought anyone before.* Two of his friends had opened the door and yelled drunkenly to him, which finally made him stop. Though she doesn't recall what they said, she took the opportunity to quickly grab her belongings. She left shoeless because she did not want to risk being trapped again.

On the walk home, Laura saw a group of her friends who were returning to their residence hall after a night out. It was the night before a semester break, so the campus was abuzz with activity even at the late hour. Laura's friends stopped and approached her. When they got close enough to see her beneath a streetlight, they immediately asked if she was okay. She could tell by their tone and worried expressions that they knew she was not. She was crying and her makeup must have been running, and, of course, there was the lack of shoes. Still, Laura assured them that she was fine and just felt really tired after a long week and evening. They asked her if she wanted to get some food with them, but she declined politely. Retreat to the safety of her room for a shower and sleep was all she wanted.

Laura showered for a long time then got into her bed and tried to sleep. Thoughts raced through her mind and kept her awake all night.

The next morning, Laura did not want to get out of bed, but she had to because of a job interview that afternoon. She really wanted the job and had hoped to impress the interviewer. Looking in the mirror, she wondered how that would be possible with a large bruise on her neck and her eyes swollen from a night of crying. She applied concealer and powder to her bruise and put on a full face of makeup. Still, she felt frozen. She was hungry, but she didn't want to go anywhere alone. She called her friend Rob, whom she had known since the first day of freshman year, and asked if he would like to meet her for breakfast.

---

* The idea of never having fought anyone before came up in two cases. Women said that they had tried to fight, but were unsuccessful. In thinking about it afterward, they weren't sure whether it was really about the relative size of the assailant or that they had never fought before and lacked the confidence to have been successful.

The unaccompanied walk to the dining hall made her feel queasy. What if she saw him? Luckily, Rob was waiting for her outside. When she walked up to him, he looked at her for a long time. She could tell that he was examining her swollen face and neck despite her efforts to hide the bruising. Rob asked her if everything was okay, and she assured him that she was fine. The two stepped into the cafeteria line and picked up their breakfast food. When they sat down at a table by themselves, Rob asked Laura what was up. Laura told him that she had gone out the night before to celebrate after an exam with some friends from her major. She said that she had had fun until the end of the night, which was "just really weird and bad." When Rob asked what happened, a description of "what happened in that room . . . not all the details, but many of them" seemed to flow out of Laura.

After telling him what had happened, Laura looked at Rob. He asked her if she was okay. He asked her, "wait, did you wanna do it?" and "did you say no?" As Laura responded to Rob's questions, she began to realize that what she had experienced was not only "weird and bad" but that it was sexual assault. ∎

Like Laura, most of the women in the project said they did not immediately place a label on what had happened to them. Rather they described experiences as Laura did when she said that *it* was really weird and bad. They communicated three primary reasons for hesitating to apply a label: (1) shock, (2) general difficulty with the formal labels of sexual assault and rape, and (3) concerns about the legitimacy of their experiences in relation to how the formal labels are applied. Some women wondered whether the level of physical force used against them or the severity of their resulting injuries would "qualify" them for the labels of rape or sexual assault. Often, they pondered such questions from a state of post-traumatic shock. One woman who said that she was still working to "come to terms with *it*" shared, "I was so just like in shock . . . I didn't believe it and I still have a hard time thinking about it as rape 'cause I, like, don't really know, that it just has such a violent connotation to it in my mind and I don't think *it* was violent but it was like . . . I know that's what *it* was."*

---

* This woman talked about the level of violence used against her in relation to the crime of murder among other violent acts.

The generic *it* was frequently substituted for experiences of sexual violence. Although the project focused on post-assault agency and interview questions did not inquire about the details of attacks, almost every woman shared specifics after I asked the initial question ("Please tell me about the experience that led you to volunteer for this project"). As we spoke, I mirrored back each woman's language choices and shifted term-use with them (for example, if a woman used the term "it" to describe an incident, I used the term "it" in the follow up). Use of the "it" label was more common during the earlier portions of interviews and in conversations with women who had experienced sexual violence on campus more recently. For example, in one interview with a woman who had experienced campus rape only a few weeks prior to the interview, the term *it* was the only descriptor used. Another woman described many specific details of the hours prior to an attack including a thorough description of the house and room that she was in. Then she said, "that's where *it* happened. I don't know if you need details or . . . ?" In addition to the term "it," many women also couched formal labels of rape and sexual assault with "softer," less-formal terms including "that thing" and "something bad."

Marla's Story

When Marla arrived at the University's counseling center, she had not slept in several days and was a self-described wreck. She had told a friend that "something bad happened," but didn't share many specifics because she did not have the right words to name her experience. She felt afraid to call the counseling center, so her friend had made the appointment for her that morning. She hoped to feel up to going to class afterward.

A kind person at the front desk greeted Marla and handed her an intake form attached to a clipboard and a pen. Marla walked slowly to a chair in the waiting area and glanced around, she was thankful that no one she recognized was there. She looked down at the form and began to fill it out. Name, Student ID number, Reason for visit . . . She didn't know what to write for the reason for her visit. After several minutes of thought, she finally wrote, "For all intents and purposes, I was raped." Her hand shook as she wrote that phrase, she looked around again worried that someone had seen her. Prior to that moment, she had only told her friend that "something bad happened," but now she was looking at the word "raped" penned in her own handwriting on the page in front of her. ■

When reflecting on her story in the interview, Marla said, "the most spectacular part of all of that was that it did not hit me . . . for like a couple of days . . . maybe two or three days." She hadn't slept and she had spoken with a friend, but she hadn't applied a label to her experience other than "something bad." Another woman who was raped had a similar experience at the student health center. She said that she had "refused to label *it*" for a long time, but when she was at the health center and the information sheet asked the reason for her visit, she felt she had to write *something* that reflected what had happened, so she wrote, "basically, I was raped." In doing so, both women added phrases that signified that they had experienced rape, but added comments to qualify the statement.

These two stories also illustrate something else these women had in common: labeling incidents of campus sexual violence was rarely static. More often, applying a label to such experiences was a process. I went into the project wondering what labels women apply to these experiences and how labels impact their actions. However, after a few interviews, I learned that these questions were far too simplistic. Rather, the labels that women used to describe incidents of campus sexual assault almost always changed or evolved over time. Yet, while the labels and time frames varied, there was a similar labeling pathway that occurred in most cases. The pathway ranged from signals like crying or repeating a phrase indicative of not having given consent (for example, "I didn't want it to happen") in the immediate context, to labeling an experience as a mistake or blocking it completely, to using the term "sexual assault" and for some, when they believed that term applied, using the word "rape." While the pathway was often similar, the process varied in length and did not always end the same way.

For most women, a major turning point in the naming process occurred when they first disclosed the experience to a trusted person (peer, parent, sibling, coach, and, in one case, a college administrator). One woman said that she called her friend and described her disclosure as "really much more of a I-don't-know-what-happened" type of thing. She said that after sharing what had happened and processing what had taken place, she knew she had experienced sexual assault, but she still doesn't use the label. Additionally, she said that her experience meets the state's formal definitions of rape, but she really dislikes the word and so chooses not to use it. Her story reminds us that while labeling can be viewed as a process, it is not always linear. It can cycle back and forth between signifiers and there is no correct pathway. Another woman in her junior year succinctly explained the progression: "I couldn't really believe it the first couple of days. And then I'd say sexually assaulted or just I wouldn't—I still wouldn't be able to label it rape or I'd just say, like I had a hard time accepting the word . . . and now I can say raped." She uses the word *can* to describe her use of the word, implying a progression and level of capability that she did not previously have. Other women echoed her sentiments about capability and progress.

Disclosure

In Laura's story, Rob played an essential role as the first person that she told about the incident. He listened to her story and asked questions in a nonjudgmental way that helped her to make sense of what had happened to her. Like Laura, the majority of the women in the project reported disclosing incidents of campus sexual violence to informal support providers such as friends and family members. Peers were the most frequent recipients of initial disclosures: this aligns with previous research.[2] In fact, within forty-eight hours, six women talked with peers, three told their boyfriends, and four told their mothers.

Women often described peers as crucial in the process of understanding what had happened through listening and sometimes scaffolding (that is, asking a series of clarifying questions that helped women process their experiences). Like Laura, another woman called her boyfriend the morning after an attack and said that she "had sex with someone else." Her boyfriend asked, "by choice or what?" at which point she began crying hysterically. Right then, she felt that the two of them reached mutual understanding about what had happened. Although she said that she continues to struggle to call what happened rape, she believes that her boyfriend could tell by the sound of her voice that she had not consented, which prompted him to ask the clarifying question about *choice*. In doing so, he gave her a platform to disclose to him without directly applying a label. Other women described similar encounters with boyfriends whether in person or on the phone.* The pattern of reaching out echoed throughout

---

* Although female-female sexual assault does occur, and I didn't assume heterosexuality among participants, all the women who took part in this study were assaulted by men and discussed telling boyfriends specifically rather than significant others.

many of the narratives. The women often contacted someone without specifying the desire to talk and, in some situations, with no intention of talking about their experience. They then ended up describing their experience or giving clues to express that something negative had happened. A series of questions from a peer followed, and then a label was applied. Thus, women often made conscious decisions about whom to reach out to, but they did not always intend to disclose until the situation presented itself.

Trusted Male Peers

It is interesting to note that in both this project and in the pilot project that preceded it, more than half of the first disclosures described by women were made to male peers. Not all of the male peers were romantic partners; some were described as trusted friends. Three women sought out trusted male peers within an hour of escaping attacks while others approached male peers between six hours and one month later. In two situations where women approached trusted male peers within an hour of an attack, women said very few words about what had happened, but the meaning was implied. For example, one woman walked to her friend's room and said, "I feel so dirty" as she cried. She told me that she didn't disclose the specifics of what had happened, but she believed that he knew from her expression.

Just as the narratives were heterogeneous, so, too, were responses to first disclosures. While I did not speak with those who heard the disclosures, women described responses from their own perspectives. In most cases, women said their male peers were comforting and tried to be supportive, but it seemed they did not know precisely what to do.* For instance, a woman who was a former resident assistant (RA) went to the residence hall room of one of her colleagues for support directly following an attack. He hugged her and rubbed her back, responses that she found supportive at the time. Later reflecting on that moment, she recalled that they had been trained as RAs together and had been advised not to touch someone who had recently been attacked. However, she thought his reaction was helpful. Other women said they did not want to be touched. Some women appreciated peers asking questions and others were grateful for

---

* Imogene's boyfriend's response was an outlier.

silent support. This highlights not only the importance of the roles played by peers, but also the importance of active listening skills and the differences in what individuals experience as helpful and supportive.

Telling Family

Two women described telling their mothers about their experiences before they told anyone else. In one case, a woman moved quickly through the stages of labeling and informed her mother over the phone that she had been raped. The other case followed a pattern similar to telling peers. The woman called her mother and, upon hearing her voice, started to cry. All she could say was, "I told him that I didn't want to. I told him I didn't want to." While she had not labeled the experience yet, her mother provided a scaffold of questions by gently asking what had happened, to which the woman replied, "I told him I didn't want to, Mom, and I'm, like, I'm so sorry." Eventually her mother asked, "Did somebody rape you?" to which she responded, "I told him I didn't want to" and finally, after several similar rounds, the woman replied, "yes." Later she told me, "I couldn't even say the word." This theme of unspeakable labels, specifically difficulty with the terms rape and sexual assault, was apparent in almost every narrative.

Deferred Disclosure

Bettina, who was raped by her friend Will, did not speak about what had happened to her for several months. One night, she was talking with her friends and began sharing the story. She described herself "telling it like it was *just* another crazy story. I wasn't telling it like something bad happened; like I was telling it like, 'Yeah, you know and then he put a t-shirt in my mouth . . .'" Her tone was matter-of-fact until she looked at her friends' faces as they listened and she started to cry. She continued telling the story, and as they responded with looks of empathy, she processed what had happened in a different way than she had previously. She had known all along that what had happened "wasn't right," but her friends' expressions confirmed her feeling.

Revisiting Georgia's Story

Georgia, the student athlete who had to see the man who attacked her frequently in the dining hall and athletic facilities, had a unique perspective on disclosure. At first, she did not want to tell anyone within the athletic department what had happened because she did not want to disrupt anything (she sought to maintain homeostasis within the system). After a few weeks, her concern that the perpetrator might attempt to assault another student led her to come forward. She decided to tell one of her coaches what had happened. She said that she was fortunate in a way that not all students at the University were because in her coach she had a representative of the college who knew her well and vice versa. She knew her coach would listen to and believe her because the coach had known her since before she came to college and understood that she would never fabricate a story of this sort. Likewise, she trusted her coach and she recognized that in disclosing to her she would not lose control of the situation: her coach would talk with her and they would decide together how to proceed. Georgia did not want to press charges through the institution's board or through the legal system, but she wanted to ensure that the man who attacked her would not assault another student. Working through her coach, the man's coach was alerted about the incident, and Georgia felt that she had made an effort to act in protection of others.* ∎

Responses to Disclosures

A 2007 study found that "survivors who actively sought help from informal support providers tended to receive positive reactions whereas survivors who sought help from formal support providers tended to receive negative reactions."[3] Friends and family were included in the definition of informal support providers. Although responses to disclosures were not the focus of this project, some women reported that other people's responses played a role in their decisions. The findings of the 2007 study held true for informal support providers: whether intending to seek support or not, the majority (but not all) of the women in the project received positive reactions upon disclosure. In contrast with the findings of the 2007 study, direct reactions from formal sources were not typically perceived as negative: counselors were found to be very helpful as were some faculty and staff members.

---

* The perpetrator left the University shortly after this event, but Georgia was never told why or what happened within the athletic department. She only knew that her coach had told his coach.

Transitive Agency

It is noteworthy that male friends were more frequently cited as aids in scaffolding toward formal labels, but female friends were mentioned more often as guides in post-assault actions (including bringing women to the emergency room or calling to make counseling appointments). Either way, the act of reaching out to someone who then functions as a bridge to a resource is an exercise of transitive agency, or agency *through* (or with the aid of) another source. Women used agency of this form for physical safety, to create a barrier between themselves and perpetrators, and, in a few cases, to access formal resources such as the emergency room, student health center, or counseling services.

"Please walk me home"

Many women worried about their physical safety in the moments following attacks. For several women, these concerns lasted for months. Peers played a significant role by accompanying women as they moved about on campus and in the local community. Being escorted by a peer provided many women with a sense of security, both physical and emotional.

In the immediate post-assault context, these connections began with phone calls or visits to peers the women perceived as trustworthy—those willing and able to help them get out of the situation and home safely, sometimes, without asking too many questions. One woman, who was raped in the bathroom of an off-campus apartment, described being left by her assailant on the tile floor of the bathroom. As she lay there, she called a male friend and, when he did not answer, she left what she described as "the worst voicemail ever." The message said, "He's coming back, he's coming back. Please come get me. He's gonna do it again, like I can't, you know, whatever." Eventually, a friend did arrive to walk her home. Other women called friends to ask them to escort them out of the spaces where they were attacked. Because most of the assaults took place at night, many of the women had to call a few people before someone picked up the phone. No one in the project described a peer bystander who intervened intentionally to stop an attack, but a few peers did seem to unintentionally disrupt (by entering the space or knocking on the door).

Naomi's Story

Naomi was with her friends at a fraternity party. A member of the fraternity began talking to her. He coaxed her into a private bedroom in the house, and the two began kissing. When things began going too far for Naomi's comfort, she asked him to stop. He refused and, though she continued to cry and begged him to stop, he raped Naomi. When he was finished, he got dressed and left the room. Naomi remained in the bed, naked and crying.

Moments later, the door opened and Naomi saw a female form enter the room. Naomi was startled and confused. The woman leaned over, picked up Naomi's clothes and said, "you need to leave. Are these your clothes?" Naomi nodded. The woman handed her the clothing and proceeded to pick up the rest of Naomi's things from the floor and hand them to her as she dressed herself. The woman told her that the man Naomi had been in the room with had a girlfriend, and he didn't want his girlfriend to know what had happened in his room, so he sent this woman to get Naomi out. When Naomi was dressed, the woman asked her if she knew how to get home, but being relatively new to campus, she did not. The woman then asked Naomi if she was okay and, although she thought she might throw up because she felt so disgusted about what had happened, Naomi just said, "yes." Naomi said that in that moment, she felt like a "zombie" as this woman helped her navigate the situation.

The woman led Naomi to a small, office-like room across the hall where there were a couple of members of the fraternity who were sober. The woman told the guys that Naomi needed a ride to campus. They stood up and led her outside to a car. Naomi got in the car with them and sat in the backseat. As they made the short trip to campus, she texted a friend and asked her to meet. She told the driver where she would meet her friend, and he dropped her off and drove away. Her friend arrived shortly after and walked her back to their building. ■

Upon reflection in her interview, Naomi said she felt "lucky" that the woman sent to get her out of the bedroom was as nice to her as she was. She also said that she later learned that it was a requirement of the Greek community to have designated sober people at every house party so that they can drive people home and help if there is an emergency. In this way, Naomi experienced a systematically planned peer response to a negative incident. Although it *was* technically a peer response, it could also be viewed broadly as an institutional response, since the Greek community enforced the sober-party-chaperones rule. Naomi said that she chose to ride home with the sober chaperones because she wanted to get to campus safely and was afraid to walk alone in the dark: she was also exhausted.

In addition to walking or driving women home so that they would not be unaccompanied, peers also took on other roles in the days, weeks, and months that followed attacks. Women described feelings of hypervigilance and fear.* When expressing these feelings, they said things like: "I felt like I saw him everywhere"; "I realized that, you know . . . I don't like to be touched anymore by anybody else . . . I am afraid to be touched"; "I was too afraid to go out and do anything [on campus] or around [campus] because I was afraid of seeing him so I just stayed in my apartment for the entire year last year." These feelings were particularly severe because in most cases women were attacked by peers at the University, meaning that the perpetrators went to the same dining facilities, classrooms, gyms, and other public spaces as the women. In a few cases, the women knew that the perpetrator was in their classes or labs, and in other cases women were surprised to see them in their classes at the beginning of a semester and were left to decide whether to remain in the course or withdraw. Even if they did not come into direct contact or the woman did not know what the perpetrator looked like,† in most cases, the fear of seeing or otherwise coming into contact with the perpetrator or his friends remained.

In an effort to negotiate these fears, many women asked peers, most commonly close friends, to accompany them as they went from place to place. For some of the women, walking across a crowded quad in the middle of the day was terrifying, and they did not wish to face that alone. One woman said, "when I finally left [my building] . . . like I couldn't do it without walking with people, with other people like good friends, like, very close, like, *physically* close to me." Another woman said that she often

---

* Hypervigilance is associated with posttraumatic stress disorder (PTSD) and is a symptom indicating increased arousal in the *Diagnostic and Statistical Manual of Mental Disorders (DSM)*.

† In one case, a woman was raped outdoors in the dark by someone who was at a fraternity formal. Based on his presence outside near the formal, she assumed that he was also a student, but she could not identify him so she did not know for sure.

thinks she sees the man who attacked her, and that the few friends who knew about the incident once "got in a little circle. . . . My friends were like, we're leaving . . . Like right now." Descriptions of friends forming a physical barrier and contributing to a sense of safety were common.

The Emergency Room

Three of the women who participated in the project went to the emergency room and twenty-three did not. Shock and the need for self-care were the two primary reasons that women decided *not* to go to the ER. A few of the women who did not elect to go to the ER spoke about their decision as though they had done something wrong. Several of them referred to the importance of physical evidence; the lack of evidence in their cases (since they had showered or slept) played a role in their decisions not to press charges through the institution. For many women, the choice not to go to the ER and the option of pressing charges were mutually exclusive in practice, though in policy they may not be. As Diana's story shows, physical evidence does not always aid in rendering a guilty or responsible finding because the question of consent still remains. It is also critical to note that strangers raped two of the three women who elected to go to the ER. This echoes previous studies that have found stranger rape more likely to be reported than acquaintance rape. [4]

Of the women who went to the ER, all went with at least one peer. Not only did peers respond themselves or support women's responses, sometimes they acted as a bridge between women and formal support services like the hospital, counseling center, health center, and others. In all of the three cases, the women said that their peers were the ones who encouraged them to seek emergency services and supported them through these experiences. Olivia described her friend Jill's role like this:

> Um, I mean there's really not anything you can say immediately after that . . . like I couldn't cognitively process at all. So having somebody try to talk to me, I mean I don't really know, like, what I needed at that point, but just knowing that I had somebody there, just like physically, was just, you know, nice to know. So, I mean, I guess, I guess, that was helpful like in a crisis moment . . . to know that I had somebody . . .

Olivia went on to describe what transpired at the ER.

Olivia: I mean, Jill, well, ninety pounds as she is, she's like leading me by the arm . . . And I, like, have my clothes in a paper bag, and I just, I couldn't function.

Lauren: How did you know to put your clothes in the paper bag?

Olivia: Um, I don't know where. Um, I volunteered, well, I used to, before all this happened and I realized I couldn't. Um, I volunteered for a crisis hotline.

. . . .

Olivia: Jill didn't really say anything. She just sat there and, like, held my hand and, like, she, like, I don't know; Jill is not really the kind of person to talk about feelings that much. Like we're very, very close, but we didn't like spend a good deal of time, like, swapping tragedy stories, or anything like that. So, I think, she was just so taken aback by, and she'd never had to deal with anything like that before, that she just didn't really know what to do.

Similarly, Penny told me about the role her friend Liz played:

Penny: My friend Liz took me to . . . um . . . the ER.

Lauren: And what was that experience like?

Penny: Um . . . that was tough. Um . . . it was really, really long and the people that, the SANE [sexual assault nurse examiner] nurse was not as . . . the ER and that was stressful because there was the, like, discussion of whether I needed to be, like, tested or immunized. I can't remember what it is for, like, HIV-AIDS and there's that whole discussion. It took forever. The nurses were not very helpful. They're like, they put me in a, I got in very quickly which was nice. Um . . . I got into a personal room . . .

. . . .

Penny: I got into my own room. Liz was there with me. I was there by my like—It was just the two of us in a room and that was really nice to have, like, our own personal space because that was when I first, I think that was the first time that I got really upset again after that first time . . . um . . . and . . . um . . . the doctor was nice but I think had a lot of other things going on understandably . . . um . . . but the SANE nurse was helpful when she finally could come in . . . um . . . and then she had talked to me about a decision that I wanted to make and that I was like, "Can I just have five minutes to think about it?" And she left and I talked to Liz about it, called my mom, and then by 10:00 we asked to have her back. The nurse, the person like helping us didn't go get her and then like forty-five minutes later, she was gone. She left and got home already and, like, it just, it was three hours in the ER that were frustrating and exhausting and I felt like, I was like recounting the story. And I knew to expect that but . . . um . . . and the decisions were like, I mean, they are hard decisions to make and the SANE, like, when she came in, for the fifteen minutes that she came in, she was wonderful . . . and very helpful and very understanding in a way that I think the doctor was sort of like, "Ugh!" I'm just a little bit uncomfortable with the whole situation and he tried to be as helpful as he could but I don't think he knew quite how to address it and that was understandable too but . . . um . . . I wanted the SANE nurse and she wasn't there and the people that, I remember Liz was so angry because she, like, kept opening the door to see if the girl had gone to get someone and she, like, opened the door twice and the girl was on, like, Facebook on the computer and Liz was like, "ugh!"

It is worth noting that in all three cases where a woman went to the ER, the peer who encouraged her to go and accompanied her was female. At the University, male- and female-identified students were trained differently about what to do in the case of an assault. Male students received very little formal education about responding, while female students received formal training that included a protocol for preparing and going to the ER (don't wait, don't shower, put your clothes in a paper bag, etc.).

Once at the ER, some women worried about paying for the tests and others worried about whether parents might be able to see the charges on credit card bills. One student found the payment for forensic testing prohibitive. She did not want to use her parents' insurance for fear the charge would show up on their bill and, like many women who were interviewed, she did not want to disclose the incident to her parents immediately. Other women worried about the costs associated with STI testing, even if the testing was done at the University's health clinic or the local public health clinic. One woman tried to get a ballpark figure for the cost of testing by searching the web. For these women, ambiguity about the cost and funding of medical exams added stress to already trying situations as payment and disclosure to family were often linked.

In sharing their stories with friends and family, many of the women in this project worried that they were burdens to them. They weighed their need to disclose and seek support against their desire to "protect" the people that they cared about. Often, telling friends or family members was an important moment in women's healing, but it was not always easy. However, it is through collective action, engagement, and remembering that we can begin to make a difference.

Judith Herman wrote:

> It is very tempting to take the side of the perpetrator. All the perpetrator asks is that the bystander do nothing. He appeals to the universal desire to see, hear, and speak no evil. The victim, on the contrary, asks the bystander to share the burden of pain. The victim demands action, engagement, and remembering.[5]

5

Seeking Justice

"I felt like telling my story to a bunch of administrators wouldn't really mean anything."

"Beware of [student name], he doesn't take no for an answer" was scrawled on the wall of a basement bathroom in the library at Brown University. In the following weeks, other students added names of men who had assaulted them to the growing list of perpetrators of campus sexual assault. As Brown's "rape-list" developed and captured national attention, custodians painted over the list to erase it from view. Women then re-created the list in a cycle of erasing and re-creating that lasted until the university opened a dialog about campus sexual assault and justice between administrators and students. The year was 1990.

In May 2014, *Bluestockings Magazine* published a piece about contemporary "rape lists" on bathroom walls at Columbia and Brown Universities and discussed the twenty-five-year history of such lists. Again, women are writing and universities are erasing: a vivid metaphor for sweeping campus sexual violence under the rug and removing it from public view. One way that Brown and other universities have responded to public attention being focused on campus sexual assault is to call together task forces to examine the issue. These groups are charged with presenting possible solutions. Brown had task forces in 1990 (around the time the Clery Act was being discussed and signed) and in 2007 (when amendments to the Clery Act were being discussed). These task forces informed institutional responses and worked to establish education and prevention groups.[1] University leaders, including those at Brown and the University that the women in this project attended, have issued "no tolerance" statements and policies. Yet students continue to experience problems with campus adjudication processes, and few of the women I spoke with perceived such systems as effective in obtaining justice.

Stories about the ways in which students have been re-victimized by university sexual assault adjudication systems include a recent case at Hobart and William Smith Colleges that was covered by the *New York Times*. A student named Anna shared her thoughts in a video testimonial on the *Times'* website,

> When I came forward, I felt so good because I was told that people had my back, they believed me, and that the right thing would be done. To look back on that now, it's just like, "why would you say that? How could you say that?" When I read the hearing, I was like, "they already had their minds made up."

According to the *Times*, the hearing, which ended in not responsible findings, began before results of the medical examination were known. Anna was questioned about reports by the police that she had not been given, and her testimony was interrupted by panelists. Additionally, medical records indicating the extent of her physical injuries were not shown to all panel members. During the review process, the accused students were ordered not to contact Anna, but one violated the order. It was not until five months later that he was found responsible for this violation, and Anna was never told whether he was punished for the infraction. Further, Anna's privacy was not protected in the process: her name was given to students who might have been asked to testify. In another case at Hobart and William Smith, a student was found responsible for sexual assault, but owing to poor questioning by the panel, his punishment was reduced upon appeal.[2]

Lena Sclove, who like Anna experienced campus sexual violence and pressed charges through her institution, Brown University, described it as a "scary place" in 2014. She accused a student and former friend of attacking her. Lena described her experience: "I was really sort of encouraged that reporting to the university is much safer than going to the police and pursuing a criminal case . . . I was not treated terribly during the hearing, but at the same time, I was not kept safe." The hearing date was set for two months after her report, meaning that she and the perpetrator were on campus together during those months. Ultimately, Brown's adjudication panel found the student responsible for the offenses and suspended him for one year. Lena appealed the decision, noting that the stated penalty was a two-year suspension. If the assailant returned to campus after one year, they would again be attending school together, a situation Lena found intolerable. The student who was found responsible released a statement on April 26, 2014, in which he withdrew his request to return to campus.[3]

Like Brown's task forces, an advisory group charged with keeping administrators up to date on issues related to campus sexual assault exists at the university studied in this project. The members of the group are appointed through the Student Affairs department, and committee work occurs annually. As at Brown, there is a board process for hearing cases of sexual assault and misconduct among students. Like Lena and Anna, the students I spoke to at the University who elected to press charges initially felt supported and believed by administrators. Diana and the two other women in the project who pressed charges were encouraged to do so. One of the women met with a dean to inquire about taking time off and was emboldened by that conversation to press charges though such action had not been on her mind prior to the meeting.[4] She said that she found the dean's support very helpful. Often women described very positive one-on-one encounters with administrators, but their perceptions of institutional representatives as a group were different.

After her experiences pressing charges through the University's board, Diana said, "now I'm going to press charges civilly because *the school doesn't care*." Recall that Diana had, in her words, done everything "by the book." She and one of the other women who had pressed charges sought help both from the authorities ("I am going to tell the police . . .") and at the emergency room within forty-eight hours of being assaulted, behavior that aligns them with the perfect victim icon. Both women had forensic tests administered in the ER. Both said they believed that having had such testing done, as well as talking with detectives and SANE nurses in the direct aftermath, meant that their cases had met the burdens of proof necessary to obtain guilty or responsible verdicts. The third woman who pressed charges met a dean in the aftermath of an attack and, based on their conversation, felt that she had institutional support moving forward with the case.*

---

* A fourth woman discussed pressing charges through another institution's board, since the man who attacked her was not a student at the University.

Two women in the project described their experiences with panel proceedings (one was still pending at the time of the interview). One was upset that she was asked, "Why didn't you go to the ER earlier?" She said that she had been incredibly shaken by the incident and sought privacy and security by curling up in her bed for several hours. After approximately ten hours she went to the emergency room. She described her internal monologue during the proceedings: "Look, I went freakin' ten hours later. It was like, is that not quick enough?" The panelist's question reflects the dominant narrative around campus sexual violence and a culture of victim blaming based on any actions that depart from those associated with the perfect victim icon. The local police were involved in both situations. Diana did not think the local detective did a "very thorough investigation." She described the way he treated her as "more like the suspect than the actual guy" who had attacked her.

Although one case was still pending at the time of the interviews, in the other cases brought forward at the University, none of the accused perpetrators was found responsible for wrongdoing.

Women's Understandings of the Role of the University

When Diana said that "the school doesn't care," she was referring to administrators and those associated with the formal adjudication procedures. Her statement reflects a common practice: referencing groups of people as *the* school, *the* university, or a bunch of administrators rather than differentiating between such groups and the individuals within them.

In contrast, women specifically named individuals within those structures who were helpful to and supportive of them. One of the University's deans and a representative from the dean's office were referred to by their names, but only in cases when they supported a woman before a hearing or helped women obtain academic support in the wake of attacks. Representatives from the counseling center, health center, and advocacy center were also referred to by name or personal descriptors. Here is an excerpt from an interview where a woman directly references both a dean and a counselor to illustrate this concept:

Quinn: Dean [last name] was also, you know, like they said, I [could] go to either the counseling center or the advocacy center . . . But she specifically gave me the name of [Counselor's first name] at the advocacy center.

. . . .

Quinn: Yeah, I actually stop therapy next week. I will be so sad when I don't see her 'cause I love her. Love her. She's my favorite person.

Lauren: So how long have you been seeing her?

Quinn: Um, pretty much since it happened . . .

Similarly, professors were referred to by name or personal descriptors, but only when women were speaking about positive contributions to their post-assault experiences. Such positive contributions included giving counsel and "checking in" after being informed about an assault. For example, one woman said:

I was in a lot of [intro] classes so they were big and I don't think that [the professors] really did notice but I did have one professor that was like, you know, "something's up with her" and she . . . I never told her but, you know, she called me in the office and, "so if you need extra time or anything just let me know." She was very intuitive.

This experience of a professor noting that something seemed different is similar to Georgia's experience of being connected to her coach. In both cases, employees who really knew the students linked them to the University's services. However, both students noted that with large classes or within the institution as a whole, not all students have such supportive individualized relationships.

Despite the mention of these supportive individuals, when women talked about "the University" as a whole, there was almost full agreement that, for the most part, the University *does not* do anything about campus sexual assault. After that, there were two schools of thought: the University *cannot* do anything about campus sexual assault and the University *will not* do anything about it.

The University *Does Not* Do Anything about Sexual Assault

"I haven't done hardcore research, and I really should, but I just hear about how *they* haven't expelled anyone in like thirty years," said one woman during an interview (emphasis added). A theme stated in almost all of the interviews (whether or not the women pressed charges) was that the University does not punish students for perpetrating campus sexual assault. A woman echoed the sentiment and talked about the importance of peer social networks for perpetuating group perceptions:

> I know people who did [press charges through the institution's board] and nothing happened . . . like I guess I should have tried myself, but . . . there are still a lot of people who were like, "yeah, that doesn't work, my friend tried that and the person doesn't get kicked out."

Another woman said that, based on what she'd heard from friends, "very small amounts [of campus sexual violence] are prosecuted, even smaller convicted." Most women stated that they believed there were essentially no consequences for perpetrating campus sexual violence at the University and that the rate of perpetrators being found responsible was low or nonexistent. As a result, many women said that pressing charges was a high-risk endeavor with a low chance of actually leading to justice or protection for themselves or others. Overwhelmingly, women in the project believed that the University held the power to adjudicate cases and expel (or otherwise hold accountable) perpetrators, but that no one or very few people were ever found responsible.

Women participating did not give much credence to the crime statistics that the University reported each year under the Clery Act. There were many different interpretations of the statistics: one woman suggested that she "heard that [in] the University's statistics on sexual assault . . . the comparisons that they use generally don't include bid night [the night when individuals celebrate being selected into a fraternity or sorority] because it's such a statistical outlier—like it's huge." After several women told me they thought the University's reported statistics were deflated, I began asking the question differently. Here is an excerpt from an interview where I shared the number of sexual assaults that the University had reported to the federal government during the previous year and asked for reactions:

> *Lauren:* Last year this University reported [fewer than fifteen]* sexual assaults. Do you think that number is accurate?
> *Rebecca:* No. They reported [fewer than fifteen]?

---

* I have elected not to use the exact number as it may identify the research site.

Lauren: Why, do you think that number isn't accurate?

Rebecca: Oh my gosh . . .

Lauren: Do you think that is close to accurate? Do you think it's like [one unit above or one below the number]?

Rebecca: That's not even close. It's not even remotely close. Wow.

Lauren: Do you think that is understated or overstated?

Rebecca: Completely understated.

Lauren: Okay, why do you think it is understated?

Rebecca: Because, one, I myself have heard from at least three people that were sexually assaulted last year at the University so, if I'm one person and I know that many people I'm pretty sure that the number is more than that, that's an educated guess . . . that number cannot be anywhere near as accurate as it is . . . It's just not.

Lauren: Well, what number do you think it is closer to?

Rebecca: Well at the University there are like [approximate number of students] students? I don't know, isn't the statistic one in four? I would go with 25 percent of that then and that sounds right and . . . like I said before, when you talk in front of a crowd you can see people who have been affected and it is a lot of people. It is something that is prevalent despite what the University really thinks, and yeah, it's something that I don't know . . . they need to do, they need to do something.

Rebecca's response was not unusual. More than one woman laughed when I told them the number that University officials had reported to the federal government the previous year. Multiple women said that they personally had heard of more women who experienced sexual assault on campus during that year than the number reported. About half the women who participated in the project believed the number accurately represented the number of assaults reported to the University owing to barriers to reporting. The other half said they believed the low statistics were the result of cover-ups and denial. Both groups believed that the reported number was very low compared to their perceptions of the prevalence rates at the University.

The students who discussed institutional cover-ups and denial said things like, "they [meaning University administrators] should stop lying about like how many times this has happened to someone." One woman suggested that Sexual Assault Awareness vigils should happen more than once per year to more consistently raise awareness. Another woman told me that she believed the University adjusted the prevalence statistics so that it "doesn't make them look really bad" because she thinks the rates are "really bad." Other women agreed that administrators try to make the campus appear safer than it really is.

The University *Can't* Do Anything about Sexual Assault

Some women felt the University was limited in its ability to do anything about campus sexual violence. For example, one woman said, "I think the hardest challenge is getting women to talk about it and, like, report men." A few women suggested that the administration was immobilized because women did not report incidents to them. A woman who shared this view stated:

> I think women are a lot of times scared to talk about it and I don't know that's like hard to get people who have had something like that happen talk about it but I mean obviously no one else is gonna report it so I don't know I mean I don't how you change the culture it's just like so like, it's so common and no one like blinks an eye when that happens like in that community and I don't know how you change that, I don't know . . .

Some women also believed the University was limited in its ability to "do anything" as a result of lacking physical evidence in most cases of campus sexual violence. Women referred to their own decisions related to self-care, noting that they did not come forward because, after showering, they had no proof to help the institution substantiate the case. One woman used the word "worthless" to describe cases like hers where there was no physical evidence and said that the University wouldn't be able to do anything. These perceptions and actions highlight the complexity and importance of agency. Some women believed their actions in the immediate aftermath of attacks limited the institution's effectiveness in adjudicating the crimes, so they decided not to report the cases to the school: perceptions of institutional ineffectiveness impacted the ways they decided to exercise agency.

Yet, as two cases revealed, even when physical evidence of sexual contact was available, perpetrators were not found responsible because cases require one to prove lack of consent. Additionally, a woman who went to the emergency room in the aftermath of an attack said that she thinks that "the ER needs to do something to fix up the way that they handle [cases of campus sexual assault] 'cause I think that . . . not enough people go to the ER, and part of it is because it's not a good experience."

Women also felt significant barriers to telling an administrator about a sexual assault directly. One woman, a former resident assistant, said she would never tell a dean or student affairs administrator because she didn't think that they have the power to "*do* anything." Another woman compared the dean of students' office to a principal's office and said she wouldn't go there because it would feel like she had done something wrong.

Student employees, namely resident assistants (RAs), were part of a few women's narratives, but again there was a sense that, in terms of justice seeking, their utility was limited.

> I didn't know where I could go so, because I mean I guess I could talk to my RA, but she couldn't really do anything about it, I didn't really have any physical evidence, so going to the police seemed too worthless and the University doesn't kick anybody out, so that doesn't mean anything . . .

Three perceptions about the University are embedded in her statement: (1) her RA was unable to act as an effective agent within the system; (2) physical evidence was crucial to a police investigation; and (3) the University does not expel perpetrators. Few women discussed negative interactions with individual administrators, staff, or faculty, but many had negative perceptions of "the University" as a whole when it came to dealing with campus sexual assault.

The University *Won't* Do Anything about Sexual Assault

Although some women did not think that the University could do anything about cases of campus sexual assault, among others there was a sense that the administration was *unwilling* to do anything; that they protected male student perpetrators. One woman said that, "*they* [the administration] just kind of like want to pretend that the whole school is a big happy family" so they protect the male students. One of the women who had pressed charges told me she believed "the whole thing [hearing process] is a setup to make sure that students never get in trouble" and that several of her friends had also come to the same conclusion. Another did not press charges because she thought, "*they* would somehow warp it [her story]—to somehow be not necessarily my fault but not his fault." Similarly, a peer concluded, "the University feels like prep school and is like the boys club . . . I don't know that they would protect me."

Sexual Assault versus Academic Dishonesty

"I think it's dumb . . . cheat on an exam? and then you're kicked out . . . And you can rape someone and then it's like, 'See you on Monday,'" one woman explained, relaying her sense that the institution's adjudication system worked for academic dishonesty but not sexual assault. Comparisons between the University's policies about academic integrity and sexual assault, particularly how differently the two were enforced, were common in interviews. Despite the fact that panel deliberations and findings were supposed to be confidential, most women agreed that no one, or at least, very few people, had ever been punished for sexual violence. Yet they believed that people *were* punished for violations of the code of conduct that applies to academic integrity. One woman succinctly stated this as, "I don't think a guy's ever been kicked out of the University for raping someone, but they get kicked out for cheating on exams." Another woman said, "*they* are going to expel two people a year for issues with academic integrity . . . if our policies are so stringent for plagiarism, I feel like they should be even more so for sexual assault."

The Choice *Not* to Press Charges

Of the twenty-six women who participated in this project, twenty-two elected not to press charges through the University.* There were three primary and inter-connected reasons for not pressing charges. First, they cited lack of physical evidence and the perception that they would not be believed as the major deterrent to utilizing the University's adjudication system. One woman said, "Like one of the main reasons I didn't report it was because I had no physical evidence whatsoever. So I felt like it wouldn't be taken seriously." Other women said they did not trust that a "he said / she said" case would end in a guilty verdict or a finding of responsible. Further, one woman explained, if the perpetrator is a student and you "don't have

* One woman was considering charges at another institution.

a cut and dry, like he jumped out of the bushes and pinned me down and raped me, then you've got no case." Another shared that "it's not like it was some stranger I guess," of a peer who raped her in her residence hall room. Unfortunately, over eighteen years after she wrote it, Robin Warshaw's quote still rings true, at least in relation to perceptions of institutional adjudication structures: "because of [rape myths], the reality of acquaintance rape is largely ignored."[5]

A second reason that women did not report the crimes to adjudication boards was concern for the perpetrators. Many of the perpetrators were peers at the University; some had been acquaintances, friends, or people with whom the women had been romantically involved. "I don't want to kick him out of the University or like ruin his life because of this," said one woman. Another said:

> I mean I hate him, but I don't. It's too beneath me to want to ruin his life either . . . so I don't like hope that he never gets with a girl again or whatever the case may be. And I don't hope that all of his friends hate him. I just hope that in some form or fashion, they recognize what happened . . . so in that way, I guess that would be my justice.

Many of the women worked for restorative justice on a personal level rather than involving the institution. This was especially the case when the perpetrator was a male peer whom the woman knew well, considered herself friends with, or with whom she was involved in the same social network (fraternity/sorority connection, same student organization, etc.).

Finally, as noted previously, many women did not perceive the University's board as effective. Sexual assault cases brought to the board require confidentiality and, at the University, both parties must sign confidentiality agreements. Thus, the majority of students (other than those who sit on the panels) are not privy to the actual number of cases of sexual assault that are brought to hearings or the number of students found responsible for such crimes. However, perceptions are very important in closed and tightly knit communities like the University, and the overwhelming belief among women in the project was that the adjudication board had *never* found anyone guilty of / responsible for sexual misconduct or assault. As mentioned earlier, many women did believe that the University's board on other crimes had found students guilty of academic dishonesty and acted in punishment. Despite no published statistics from the board, there was a perception that it was ineffective. One woman explained a view that was held by most of the women with whom I spoke:

> I would have [pressed charges with University's adjudication board] if the school dealt with things differently because—'cause the statistics are actually pretty horrific . . . Not a single person has been suspended or expelled even when the panel found that they were guilty. That's really upsetting . . . And like—so I could put myself through this absolutely horrific experience of having to go confront him in front of a bunch of people and tell a huge group of people what happened and nothing has happened to him at all . . . So it just kind of punishes me more and he gets a little slap on the wrist.

Almost every single person with whom I spoke expressed some form of the idea that guilty verdicts / responsible findings are either extremely rare or have never been handed down. On top of that, the overwhelming belief among women in the project, both those who had pressed charges and those who had not, was that it is a negative experience (horrific, terrible, awful, worthless) that would not bring closure because the perpetrators would not be found responsible. One woman suggested that: "the whole thing is a set-up to make sure that students never get in trouble."

Taking Justice into Their Own Hands
Throwing a Punch

Sabrina's Story

Sabrina, a senior, was enjoying her first date with a graduate student from the University. The two had gone out to dinner, visited the bars near the University, and then decided to continue the evening at a party hosted by one of the local fraternities. They walked into the party, picked up some drinks, and were talking to a few of Sabrina's friends when Sabrina thought she noticed a familiar face in the crowd. She asked her date to excuse her for a moment.

Sabrina walked across the dim room toward a couple that was dancing. She gently pushed the female student out of the way and looked at the young man. "Excuse me, are you Ted Tarquin [not his real name]?" Sabrina was careful to ask for his first and last name. When he said yes, Sabrina punched him directly in the face.

Ted had raped Sabrina at a party the previous semester. Because the room was dim and there were many male students who looked similar to Ted, Sabrina wanted to be sure that she "followed up" with the right man. Once she knew that it was, in fact, Ted, she punched him. ∎

When Sabrina told me this story, she did so in a matter-of-fact way. She described punching Ted as "very liberating" and as "exacting [her] own type of revenge." Yet, punching Ted in the face was not something she had pre-planned. Rather, she said that, "for a long time, whenever [she] saw him, [she'd] just flip out . . . [she] would just freak out" with worry and fear.

Punching Ted in the face felt "liberating" for Sabrina. In doing so, she joined the ranks of about one-third of the women who operated outside of official legal or institutional judicial systems in their work toward closure and justice. The reasons that women took justice into their own hands were varied, yet five significant themes emerged: (1) they were socially linked to the perpetrator (as co-workers, friends, classmates, etc.); (2) they weren't sure the perpetrator understood the depths of the pain they had caused; (3) they worried about other women who would interact with the perpetrator in the future (would he rape another woman?); (4) they did not necessarily trust that the institutional or legal system would properly handle their cases; (5) they wanted the perpetrator to be punished, but they didn't want to "ruin his life" as they felt expulsion would. All felt that going through the University's system or the legal system would strip them of the power to make their own decisions about the process, but all felt they needed to do something and that the burden of action was entirely on them. This is one of the pieces of the story of campus sexual violence that is missing from public conversations. There has been news coverage about legal and institutional "justice" mechanisms, but very little has been said about electing to work toward closure outside of these formal systems. Women's stories revealed their motives and perceptions of the outcomes from these actions.

Writing a Letter

Tina's Story

Tina worried that the former friend who had raped her would rape another person. She was distraught as she balanced the anxiety associated with seeing him, her concerns about the judicial system at her school (to her knowledge, no one had ever been convicted of sexual assault and punished), and the guilt she would feel if she didn't *do something.*

She also felt that she had not acted properly in the hours following the assault. She was exhausted and upset and wanted to shower, so she did not go to the emergency room to have evidence collected. In addition, she questioned whether evidence could prove anything other than that sex had taken place. She had heard stories of women who had rape kits done and still hadn't been successful pressing charges because the physical evidence didn't prove lack of consent.

The perpetrator had been her friend. If she did press charges, it would ruin his life. He would never be able to get a job. In fact, it would probably ruin her life too: she might never get a job if people thought she was a liar or a troublemaker or even just associated her with a campus rape.

There was much to consider and Tina just wanted to move past the anger, hurt, and fear. Yet, as days passed, she became increasingly afraid that he would attack another person and her guilt grew.

Partly Tina wanted to talk to him: tell him how he had hurt her and implore him not to do the same thing again. She wanted to be able to see his face so that she could tell whether she had made an actual impact. However, she feared that, in his presence, she would not be able to find the words to fully explain her feelings. It had taken her weeks to even put words to the experience and tell a friend. Her friend had connected her with the advocacy center on campus and a counselor who helped her figure out what to do next.

Finally, Tina decided she had to act, so she wrote a letter to the perpetrator. She wrote all of the things she wanted him to know, explaining the extent of the pain he had caused her. She wrote that he had hurt her confidence and caused her to feel unsafe all of the time. She explained her feelings of hypervigilance, her difficulties sleeping, and how she struggled to keep up in classes. She closed by writing that she hoped that he would never do anything like that to another woman.

Next, Tina texted him; they had been friends before the incident so she had his number in her phone. She asked if they could meet and scheduled the meeting in a public space away from where the attack had occurred. She did not want to be alone with him.

Tina sat patiently at a table outside a bustling café in the downtown area of their town. When he arrived, she recalled, he acted as if nothing had changed between them. He even hugged her and leaned in for a kiss on the cheek, something she found very upsetting. She handed him the note and asked him to read it while she watched.

What happened next helped Tina obtain a sense of closure, but she told me almost a year later that she does not think what happened would be likely in other situations. The perpetrator looked at her and apologized. He said he was sorry for what he had done and for the pain it had caused her. He said he would never do something like that again.

Reflecting on this process, Tina realized that it was not only the apology that helped aid in her healing: the process of writing all of the ways the assault affected her was also instrumental in letting her move on. ∎

About a third of the women I talked with reported that the process of writing or otherwise articulating their feelings about being sexually assaulted (whether or not they shared them with the attacker) was important to their healing. Yet, the forms of self-defined justice or closure-seeking ranged, as did the outcomes. Sabrina punched her assailant in the face and felt a sense of liberation. Tina shared a letter and received an apology. Other women spoke with the men (one on Facebook and one in person) who had formerly been their friends and asked them not to communicate with them anymore. In both cases they were successful in ending contact.

Photographing Bruises and Other Forms of Expression

For some women, re-connecting with perpetrators and expressing themselves brought closure and liberation; other women used different types of expression to work toward healing. Private forms of self-expression also figured largely in women's narratives. Uma, for example, woke up the morning after being assaulted and "felt the need to write something," so she composed an entry in her journal that included specific phrases the assailant had said during the attack. She also took photographs of the bruises on her body. Reflecting back on the morning after the assault, Uma said, "I don't know why [I took the photos], I think maybe part of me was being rational like, if you ever wanted to do something about this, like you should have . . . some sort of [proof]." She saved the journal entry and photos on her computer and, after some time had passed, she looked at them again. She noticed that the journal entry was not long, "just like a page or something, but I, ah, it, like, actually brought back some memories of the actual incident that I had remembered, like specific sayings that he had said." At that point she decided to delete the photos of her bruises but to keep the journal entry, leaving her with her own reflections but no visual reminders. A few weeks after this, she contacted me about participating in the project.

Like Uma, Valerie used writing as a tool for healing, but she did so later in her process. In the days following an experience of sexual assault, Valerie found herself having writer's block. As a student in a writing course that semester, this was very difficult for her. Finally, she explained, she "just . . . couldn't think of anything else to write about," so she wrote about her experience of sexual violence. She "warped it a little bit" and called it a fictional story. When I asked her about the experience, she said:

> I feel like it helped to like, get it down so it was out of my head and a little bit was on paper. And also, to sort of hand it in in an anonymous sense to be work-shopped by my peers. It's like, almost because it wasn't me, but it was a character, that helped 'cause I separated from the character a little bit and also, it just like helped 'cause I felt like they were all understanding what it's like to go through it . . . not necessarily that they would look at me and be like, "Oh, that's what you're going through" but thinking more generally about like, "Oh, this is maybe what a girl goes through."

I asked Valerie how much of the "fictional account" she had submitted was real, and she said, "ninety percent, but the nice thing about fiction is no one had to know . . ."

Another woman found that writing was instrumental to her healing, but not necessarily writing about being assaulted. She said that she experienced "cyclical thoughts" about the assault for weeks afterwards, and it was difficult for her mind to focus on anything else. In an effort to give herself an outlet, she started a blog. The blog was in the public sphere so anyone could read it, and she typically wrote about music, a passion of hers. She occasionally wrote about her experiences, but in a way that was linked to music. She said that she found blogging a very helpful outlet as she worked to end the "cyclical thoughts."

Winnie's Story

Sam, the student who raped Winnie, was in a fraternity whose members frequently spent time with Winnie's sorority. Winnie had only told one or two of her closest friends about the incident and had elected not to tell anyone else. One evening, Winnie was at a party being hosted by one of her sorority sisters when Sam walked in. Upon seeing him, Winnie felt sick to her stomach. She didn't want to be in the same room as him, but she also didn't want to leave the party where she and her friends had been enjoying themselves. She didn't want to explain to the other students at the party what had happened to her. She didn't know what to do. Then, one of her sorority sisters with whom she had previously shared her experience approached her. She said, "I asked Sam to leave. He wanted to know why, and I told him he wasn't welcome here. He's pissed, but he's gone."* Winnie felt a sense of relief, she didn't have to explain, she didn't have to leave, she didn't have to see Sam. ■

Winnie's story points to the diversity among women's narratives even when contextual factors are similar. Both Imogene and Winnie were raped by male peers in fraternities with ties to their own sororities, yet while Imogene's sorority sisters did not support her, Winnie's sorority played a critical role in re-establishing her sense of security.

There were other cases where peers played a role in justice- and security-seeking outside the formal institutional or legal adjudication systems. One woman told her boyfriend, who attended a different college, about being attacked, and her boyfriend sent a message to the perpetrator through a social media platform. The message was simple: a few words saying that what the perpetrator had done was wrong. In another case, a woman described to a male peer several months later what had happened to her. Her friend was in the same fraternity as the perpetrator. A few days later, her friend told her that he "beat up" the perpetrator. Upon hearing about the fight, the woman experienced a complex set of feelings: she felt

---

* This isn't a participant quote, it is based on the way the woman told the story.

happy that there had been some retribution for his actions yet she also felt guilty that there was more violence.

Self-Defined Justice

Definitions of justice are culturally bound. While those outside of the campus and the media spend a lot of time addressing the legal and institutional judicial systems that regulate colleges and universities, there are students who work toward their own definitions of justice, either alone or with the aid of peers. Actions aimed at students' own definitions of justice are also forms of agency that must be taken into account by policy makers, administrators, and support providers. Additionally, the perceptions and motivations that impact the ways students exercise agency in the context of colleges and universities are critical. Most frequently, women in the project said they were driven to act out of concern for others, something that was magnified by being part of a campus community. For some women, participation in the project was also a form of safe self-expression and justice-seeking on an institutional level. In the space of the interviews, sitting bravely with a stranger, knowing that their identities would be concealed, women frequently said they were sharing their stories to protect other women and to work toward institutional change.

6

The Beautiful Process of Empowerment

"I would never be able to walk with somebody through sexual assault if I hadn't experienced healing."

One of the women who participated in the project used the phrase "beautiful process" to describe her role as an agent in the healing and education of others. As she supported peers in their post-assault healing processes and served as an advocate, both she and her community were strengthened. Like her, approximately half of the women in the project discussed the ways that they exercised agency in support of others and to raise awareness about sexual violence.* This form of agency can be characterized as empowerment and defined as participation in independent or collective actions that demonstrate or amplify social, political, or spiritual power. Exercises of empowered agency included organizing events for the community, speaking or presenting at awareness-raising events, researching gender violence, serving in organizations aimed at supporting other students, teaching self-defense classes, and working one-on-one with peers who have experienced sexual violence.

Organizing Awareness-Raising Events

April is Sexual Assault Awareness Month in the United States. Events, including rallies, presentations, and vigils, are held on college campuses and in communities across the country. Like many colleges, the University hosts awareness-raising and empathy-building events for the campus community during the month. These events are run by students,

---

* One notable theme was that the majority of women who spoke about exercising empowered agency had been attacked a year or more prior to their interviews: the exercise of empowered agency may occur later in the process or not at all.

faculty, and staff who work together in support of the cause. Two of the women who participated in the project discussed their roles in organizing events for Sexual Assault Awareness Month aimed at educating others about the impacts of sexual violence.

One of the women helped to organize a vigil where students could stand in a concealed space to protect their identities while sharing their stories through a microphone so that their voices would be amplified, allowing a large group of people to hear them. Attendees were given small candles to hold as they listened to the participants. The woman shared how difficult it had been to keep the candles lit one year when it was windy, but how beautiful it was to see all of the candles together in the darkness, each representing a person who had come to bear witness.

The second woman who spoke about working on a vigil event focused her narrative on the supportive atmosphere among organizers. She noted that the students, faculty, and staff collaborated well. She then named a specific University staff member employed in their advocacy center and said how working on the event had brought them in contact and how much she had learned from their time together.

Speaking or Presenting at Awareness-Raising Events

While some women planned and ran events, others participated by presenting at them. One woman talked about speaking at a panel presentation during Sexual Assault Awareness Month and then throughout the year with organizations that worked to educate other students about sexual violence. Another woman, Xena, spoke about singing a well-known song that has been helpful in her own healing into the microphone at a vigil and asking others to join her. Xena has a unique voice that she describes as "distinct." This is important because she knew that her peers would recognize her voice if she shared her story at the vigil, even if her body was concealed. Here's a brief excerpt from our conversation about telling her story at the vigil:

> At the University, I know hundreds of people, and I interact with them on a daily basis. I work with them. I go to school with them. I am in class with them. I have a distinct voice, so just because they don't know my name it doesn't mean people don't know that it's me. So honestly, a large part of it was a fear of people just looking at you differently and

treating you differently, and, or even just pitying you in some ways . . . and this is scary, not knowing what someone is thinking . . . It is really important because I don't want people to look at me differently just because I shared, it doesn't mean I am different all of a sudden . . . It was scary to be honest.

In her interview, she also described her strong Christian faith and said that she had recently been on a mission trip where she told her story for the first time to others who were not close friends or confidantes. She explained how the mission trip differed from her experience sharing her story at the University:

There was a difference between going somewhere else and doing something and doing it here [at the University] . . . it's like my home. It takes a lot more courage . . . it's a bigger deal, but it was good and the way my friends received it, even a lot of the guys, it was so encouraging. And, after that [sharing her story and song], actually there were a lot of girls that walked up to each of us . . . or emailed us or whatever, people that we knew, people we didn't know and were like, "hey I really want to talk to you." And anytime someone goes, "I want to talk to you," it's a bittersweet thing, but now it's good.

Xena explained that it is "bittersweet" when people ask to talk with her after she shares her story because it typically signals that they want to tell her their story and to seek support from her. She told me that she cherishes the role of trusted person to whom others disclose, but admits it can be difficult. At this point in our conversation, Xena began using the collective term "we" when she talked about her experiences at the vigils:

Last year, *we* spoke . . . and this year *we* spoke, and I went first. But, watching all of these girls speak, I just kind of sat there amazed because I have watched every single one of these girls through this process of healing, and it was amazing to see them, like, stand out there with courage or be terrified. One of the girls, I know that she's been sexually assaulted, but I've never talked to her about it. It's just one of those innate things that I sometimes just know. She was really relieved to see me, and I like sat with her the whole night, and she was like not doing so well, and it was really hard for her to share, but at the same time I talked to her about it afterwards and it was really good for her . . . you've stepped in to her healing . . . so over the years it's just been this beautiful process of watching people heal and healing myself.

Participating in Student Organizations

Xena and I discussed her use of the pronoun *we*, and she explained that she was part of a student-run prayer group on campus. She told me that there was a group of women who have experienced sexual violence who come together to talk and pray, and that many members of the group went to the vigil to share their stories and bear witness together.

A few other women who participated in the project also discussed the importance of this prayer group. One of them spoke to me about her leadership role in the group. She had shared the story of her experience with sexual violence at a Christian student group meeting (not a group about sexual violence), and an older student invited her into the subject-specific prayer group. This older student was the group's facilitator and became a mentor for the woman. At the time of her interview, her mentor had graduated, but the two remained in close contact. The woman became the group's new leader, and she spoke to me about how much effort she put into effectively facilitating the group in hopes of supporting other women in their journeys toward healing. She said:

> It kind of makes me want to research more and know more about God and the Bible and it kind of like helps my relationship with God grow because . . . how can you lead other people if you don't know? And counsel people if you're not in a good place? . . . So that itself has helped tremendously. It's the same thing with, I would never be able to walk with somebody through sexual assault if I hadn't experienced healing. It's just not how it works.

She had determined the theme of suffering and resilience as the group's focus for the year:

> So, this year, as far as I'm concerned, I've been looking a lot at the question of suffering and I'm like, "Okay, how does this work, God?" "What does it mean that you are the great God who created everything yet these things happen, lives are broken and destroyed and what does this

mean?" Because this is the question that was asked constantly and there's an answer I need, this is an answer so many people need too, not just me, and I think that is also, as a survivor, that's a huge question, like that's something that keeps people away from God a lot is, "Okay well how has this happened? Like you say you care about me and, you're like loving and always here, but where were you then at that moment?"

Her questions for God and those of the other women in the group led her on a search to find new resources and workbooks to share. She said that her investment in the group and in their collective and individual healing was of paramount importance in her life and that she spent hours each week preparing and planning for group meetings. She even sent Bible verses and resources for me to post on the project's private website in hopes of them being useful to other women in the University community. Also, leading the group requires her to be thoughtful about her own healing and journey because you can't "counsel people if you're not in a good place."

Researching Gender Violence

Many of the women who participated in the project had spent time thinking about how their experiences and knowledge could be used to help other students. One woman contacted me after the interview and asked if we could discuss *her* research. She told me that she and a group of her peers were concerned about a specific form of gender violence, and they wanted to study the issue further. The University, like many colleges, has a program that enables undergraduates to apply for research funds to support their work. The awards include more than funding: they connect students to training and resources. In turn, students submit a research paper for potential publication.

The student and her team assembled a very thoughtful research plan. We talked about the methods for the project, the ethics involved with interview-based research about sensitive topics, and other important research considerations. I sent them the interview protocols for this project as well as consent forms, institutional review board documentation, and recruitment wording to give them some ideas. The team applied for and received one of the competitive grants.

Over the next year, the team, led by a woman who had participated in this project, generated original research about gender violence that stands to inform the way that we think about the issues.

Teaching Self-Defense Classes

Several women in the project said that after being attacked they took self-defense classes or increased their exercise and strength-training regimens, all important forms of embodied and empowered agency. One woman said that she was in training to become certified to teach self-defense classes to other women, a form of empowered agency.

Using Their Stories for Change

At the root of every interview was the participants' intention of making things better for others by sharing their stories. Many women spoke about their desire to use something negative that happened to them in an effort to raise awareness. About half of the women spoke about feeling a sense of empowerment and engaging in actions that demonstrate or amplify their social, political, or spiritual influence.* Bettina talked about her investment in changing the institution and sharing her story in hopes of helping someone else. She said:†

> Like the whole time I was going through this I was like, I'm not a victim like I'm not. Like, I will—I refuse—because I'm only a victim if I like sit in here and cry the whole time. Like I'm not, like I need, like I have the power to change this so I will do everything in my power to make sure this doesn't happen to somebody else and—because nobody should have to go through that.

Bettina draws a contrast between her victim identity and her agent status. Rather than facing the dichotomy between the innocent sexual victim (perfect victim icon) and the "rational sexual agent," women who participated in this project described rejecting the victim label while still actively

---

* This chapter is shorter than the others because only half the women discussed empowerment, not because it is less important than the other forms of agency.

† After extensive discussion both in interviews and on the web forum, the terms *survivor* and *victim* remain contested by women. The creation of a label that better suits their desires and self-definition is a space for future work in this arena.

associating with and supporting others who occupied the position of sur-vivor/victim.

The forms of empowered agency included telling their stories publicly and telling their stories to me in private but knowing that they would be compiled and made public. Other forms were conducting research aimed at reducing gender violence on campus and leading a faith-based group for women who have experienced sexual violence. Each case reveals the power of community and connection. The women who spoke about these forms of post-assault agency *use* their politically constructed positions as victims toward the betterment of their communities and prove that victimization and agency are not polarized or fixed. After speaking with several women who were working to heal themselves and their community I realized that Xena was right when she described the "beautiful process of watching people heal and healing [her]self."

Agency and Campus Sexual Assault: The Way Forward

We "have the power to change this."

This is an important moment for anyone interested in making college campuses safer spaces. Public attention is focused on the prevalence of campus sexual violence. Brave students have come forward to share their stories about the ways in which the "justice" systems at their universities have failed them. Numerous colleges and universities are under federal investigation for possible Title IX violations related to sexual assault investigations. The White House Task Force to Protect Students from Sexual Assault issued its first report in the spring of 2014. A Senate subcommittee issued a report that found that "many institutions are failing to comply with the law and best practices in how they handle sexual violence among students. These problems affect nearly every stage of the institutions' responses to sexual violence."[1]

The women who shared their stories in this project came forward in an effort to make the University a safer place. Their experiences and perceptions include essential elements for institutional and national responses to campus sexual violence. One of the most significant messages in their stories is that post-assault agency includes more than seeking justice. Women exercise agency following attacks in many different ways, and only a few of the agency forms have been widely recognized. Women attended to their physical needs, managed their identities, expressed themselves through art, and worked to better their community. They determined whom they trusted enough to tell and in what contexts they should elect to remain silent. And just as their environment impacted their decisions, they also impacted their environment by making people more aware and working to protect other students. Women's experiences, perceptions, and behaviors were heterogeneous, but there were many shared themes. As we think about national-level reform of institutional responses, we must consider the many ways that college students exercise agency following instances of sexual violence, not just re-enforce and re-entrench the pathways of the perfect victim icon. A more comprehensive understanding of college women's post-assault agency reveals many elements that are crucial to improving national and institutional climates and responses to campus sexual violence.

Embodied Agency: Revisiting the Perfect Victim Icon

The word *victim* comes from the Latin *victima* meaning "the sacrificed ones" and implies flawlessness as well as suffering.* According to Jan van Dijk, a professor of Criminology, the term also denotes the impossibility of recovery and frames the perpetrator positively in the role of altruistic sacrifice-maker.† Perhaps a component in the struggle with the use of the term victim is the intrinsic meaning beyond its contemporary usage. The word victim never seemed to simply mean "a person who had experienced a crime." Even if the roots of the term are not known, somehow there is a tension associated with it. It seems to imply helplessness and powerlessness while at the same time holding important political weight. In looking more deeply into the history of the term, one learns that the etymology of the victim label has consequences for individuals who have experienced crime. For example, van Dijk noted that:

> Up to late medieval times, victims and their families in Europe had a right to seek revenge . . . The newly imposed moral imperative for crime victims to renounce their traditional right of revenge and/or blood money requests them to abandon a once powerful legal position in relation to the offender . . . Victims are expected to make a significant sacrifice on behalf of the community. The functionality of crime presupposes effective silencing of the victim.[2]

Thus, in cases of campus sexual assault, the "perfect victim" is defined by how others perceive her. She is expected to sacrifice her "right of revenge," or any individual-level response aimed at a concept of "justice," by silently handing off the responsibility for justice to someone else (for example, the

---

* For example, "Do not bring anything with a defect, because it will not be accepted on your behalf." Leviticus 22:20.
† After all, a sacrificial animal ultimately dies.

University's adjudication board). In doing so, her power becomes relative to how she is perceived and what others believe is "just."[3] This is one reason that women acted to manage their identities following experiences with campus sexual assault.

In the system of justice at the University and many college campuses across the United States, the choices available to the perfect victim as they relate to justice are limited, bounding her agency as well. In reporting her case, she can select whether or not to press charges. If she does not press charges, other students may remain at risk, and the attack will not be "counted" in institutional reports rendering it nonexistent from a campus safety perspective. If she elects to press charges, typically someone else examines the details of the case and determines what type of violation occurred based on the legal or institutional definitions.

If she chooses to press charges, her body and identity become the site of investigation: What was she doing before the attack? What was she wearing? How forcefully did she say no? Is there physical evidence on or inside of her? Since the perfect victim was "unblemished," chose not to shower, and immediately went to the emergency room where physical evidence was found, the case proceeds. Next, she is brought before a panel, in a room with the perpetrator, and her identity and behaviors are questioned and held against an idealized standard. Those who she told about the incident are called to testify not only about what she told them, but about their perceptions of her and her behaviors. In many ways, when she brings her case forward, the perfect victim is expected to give up much of her power and become an object within the system where she is subjected to widely accepted rape myths.[4]

So, does the current system of justice that exists in some form at most colleges and universities in the United States serve the interests of students who experience sexual violence? Based on the stories from the women in the study, it does not. A cultural shift must begin with naming and discussing the aspects of the perfect victim icon upon which such systems are based. This icon is, as the name implies, an unreasonable standard that sets up the system to fail the majority of the time. However, prevention campaigns and support projects are often aimed at the perfect victim. Students and faculty who sit on adjudication panels are often trained in how the perfect victim responds to assault. They ask questions with an idea in mind of how she would answer. Finally, students who experience campus sexual violence compare their experiences against hers to determine whether or not they deserve justice.

If we want to create a system that is supportive of people who have experienced sexual violence, we must begin to dismantle the role that the perfect victim icon plays within institutional systems of justice. The framework of justice should restore power to people who have experienced crime, not take it away or re-victimize them.

Managing Identity

The perfect victim icon was also invoked when women discussed the ways that they exercised agency to alter or maintain perceptions of themselves. Some women worked to remove elements that contributed to the sexualized gazes cast upon them by cutting their hair or changing their mode of dress because the perfect victim icon is not sexually enticing. Other women acted to preserve how they were viewed, as the perfect victim icon is rational and methodical.

An element of the perfect victim icon that is specific to the campus context is her academic achievement and identity. Women in the project were very concerned about the ways their academic achievement could be impacted by how they dealt with experiences of sexual violence. Decisions about how to exercise agency took into account fears that they would not get jobs and that faculty and administrators would view them negatively because their names would become associated with problems. Additionally, some women were concerned that the process of reporting and pressing charges would take away valuable time from their studies. Other women were challenged to balance academic identity with fear when they were enrolled in the same courses as perpetrators: they could attend class and experience anxiety or miss class and risk negative faculty perceptions of them. Worries related to academic identity are substantial and need to be considered if campuses are to be more supportive spaces for students who have experienced sexual violence.

Student Disclosure

Although the choice to remain silent is a form of agency, all of the women in the project disclosed attacks to at least one person. Women described the responses of those they chose to tell as very important in their healing trajectories. Most commonly they spoke to peers, but some spoke to parents, siblings, staff, and faculty. This underscores the importance of training and open dialogue with all of these groups of people. Such training should include the authentic voices of students as well as real-life scenarios. Students who have experienced campus sexual assault and are interested in working on awareness-raising as an exercise of empowered agency may be helpful in creating training materials.

At the University and numerous other colleges and universities, faculty, staff, and students are given information about resource providers and institutional policies. This is a good start but it does not go far enough to explain the nuances related to student disclosures, knowledge of student needs, and the available options and resources. Future training protocols can be informed by those used by institutional review boards at research universities where faculty and students who seek to conduct research are required to be trained in research ethics and show their mastery of simple ethical themes. The training protocols for researchers seeking to conduct research with human subjects typically involve information about real cases that illustrate the crucial points. Such training is required of anyone who wishes to do research on campus and can be completed online at any time. Campuses could require similar training on consent, campus expectations, and support resources. Including individuals who have experienced campus sexual violence in the creation of such training mechanisms can help make them relevant to individual campuses. Such inclusion also gives survivors a platform for empowerment and expression.

At the University, many women and the peers they spoke to in the aftermath of attacks were not aware of the full array of resources available to them. Those who were aware of the resources did not always know how to access them or what accessing them entailed. What questions would they be asked? Would the encounters be confidential? Would there be intake forms where they would be asked to write down what happened? If so, what questions would be on them? Would they have to report the incident formally? How long would they wait for an appointment? Would other people see them in these resource spaces and know why they were there? Who could they trust?

Many students in the project spoke about being pleased with the counseling and health resources available to them through the institution once they engaged with them, but a primary barrier to accessing resources was ambiguity. At the University, students were given information about the resources available to them at orientation and they were also told that the information was available online, but specific descriptions of what is involved in accessing each resource came mostly from soliciting information from peers and involved disclosure. Further, an Internet search of "sexual assault" along with the name of the school in question can often bring students not to resources but to stories of others who have had negative experiences at the institution; this was the case at the University. Institutions would take a significant step in reducing ambiguity, and thereby barriers to resources, if they posted detailed descriptions of the various resources, including details about wait times, waiting rooms, whom they will see, what can be expected in terms of confidentiality, what will be asked on intake forms, etc. Women in the project endorsed the idea of videos showing the spaces, people, and forms available at least on internal websites and several of the women said they would be willing to help create such videos. All of this should be designed to encourage use and alleviate anxiety.

Seeking Justice: Balancing Transparency and Confidentiality

The women's narratives reinforce the need to reconsider the balance between transparency and accountability on one hand and confidentiality on the other. While federal policy has focused on accountability by asking colleges and universities to report crime statistics, there is little accountability for the judicial processes on these campuses. The construct of confidentiality prohibits administrators at the University and other campuses from reporting the results of board hearings even to their own students. And while at the individual level student confidentiality must be maintained, there is nothing preventing institutions from releasing statistics on a five-year lag or otherwise aggregated to protect individuals and cases. By reporting a rate, institutions would be more accountable to their stakeholders, allowing students to make more informed decisions. In the case of the University, most of the women expressed the perception that no perpetrators brought in front of the adjudication board had been found responsible for their crimes. There is no report of findings so it is impossible to know if this is true, but the perception, coupled with the idea that they would be treated poorly by the system, played major roles in their decision-making. If colleges and universities were required to report the rates of responsible findings from all board hearings to their constituents, even aggregated or on a five-year delay, it may inform decisions. This would also hold internal boards more accountable to their findings by providing some level of transparency.

Penalties

Penalties also need consideration at both the federal and institutional levels. At the federal level, the penalty for failure to investigate issues under Title IX is the loss of federal aid to the college, but the full penalty has never been enforced.[5] The report from the Senate Subcommittee on Financial and Contracting Oversight noted that:

> More than 40% of schools in the national sample have not conducted a single investigation in the past five years. More than 20% of the nation's largest private institutions conducted fewer investigations than the number of incidents they reported to the Department of Education, with some institutions reporting as many as seven times more incidents of sexual violence than they have investigated.[6]

Thus, while the potential loss of federal funds puts entire institutions at risk, it lacks regulatory teeth, since it has not been fully enforced to date.

Likewise, the women who spoke to me at the University indicated their belief that penalties for perpetrators found responsible for campus sexual assault were rarely enforced. This finding is echoed in the media, calling into question whether the system works at all. Significant thought needs to be put into meaningful, enforceable penalties and making those penalties known to students.

Refining Institutional Responses

Seeking institutionally defined justice *is* a type of agency, but it is often the only type of agency discussed.* Institutional responses should recognize other types of agency. For example, for many students, self-care in the immediate post-assault context involves cleansing and resting. The White House Task Force calls for the development of comprehensive sexual misconduct policies. Policies of this sort must acknowledge the likely absence of physical evidence and thus, not be framed in a way that implies a reliance on it. As the cases brought forward at the University suggest,

---

* There are a few studies of other aspects of agency, namely disclosure, that are cited in chapter 4.

even with physical evidence, the crime itself often cannot be proven. This must be a significant element in conversations about sexual misconduct policies despite the challenges that it poses.

Moreover, students and alumni should be included in institutional-level policy conversations; collegiate cultures vary and the perspectives of students should be taken into account. Policy development and implementation can benefit significantly from student opinions and perceptions since they are the individuals called to engage the policies. If students do not perceive policies as effective or potentially effective, as we saw at the University, the policies will not be fully utilized.

Finding Their Own Way

Women who had been assaulted a year or more prior to their interviews frequently discussed the ways that they had exercised empowered agency to raise awareness and support others. Institutions must create or maintain opportunities for this form of agency to be exercised. Programs and staff connected with the University's advocacy center featured positively in many narratives as they facilitated the exercise of empowered agency. For example, the advocacy center staff helped organize the Sexual Assault Awareness Month activities that several women discussed in their interviews. The advocacy center also supported several campus education groups that students participated in. In an effort to continue to foster empowered agency and a culture of students supporting one another, institutions should sustain offices of this nature.

Of course, the ideal outcome of work in the arena of sexual violence is prevention. This will take a significant cultural shift that can be led by, but must not solely be the domain of, institutions of higher education. Responsibility lies partly with the K–12 system, the media, families, and those involved with social services. This underscores an important component of the conversation: although sexual assault on campus is a significant problem, sexual assault in general is a societal issue that is not the exclusive domain of colleges and universities. Prevention activities must start early and take place in many different arenas—all of which takes commitment, thought, and resources.

Colleges and universities are unique and important spaces because they are regulated, symbolic, and founded on principles of benefit to the public good. Employees and administrators at such institutions sometimes are vilified in public depictions, particularly in relation to cases of campus sexual assault. However, as the stories of the women at the University reveal, there is a divide between the faceless "institutions" and the individuals working on behalf of students within them. At the individual level, many women felt supported by faculty and staff members: they named individuals who were helpful to them. Nonetheless, when viewed as a group, experiences with "the administration" were perceived differently. This speaks to the need for a focus on a humanistic response to campus sexual violence. We need a better understanding of administrator, staff, and faculty agency and what supports and confines it.

Colleges and universities are also spaces with extensive rituals of orientation to their culture that begin long before students set foot inside classrooms. The ways in which campuses orient students should include an introduction to campus culture that centers on care, consent, and agency. Once students are on campus, prevention work should *continue* and draw on efforts from the K–12 and other social arenas. Because college is a setting for individual development and critical thought, the campus culture itself should be a topic for critical thought and discourse among students, faculty, and staff. For example, students should be challenged to think about the social norms around gender and power. On many campuses, heteronormative gender mores and expectations remain prevalent, much to the disadvantage of students. These norms would be excellent topics for building and exercising critical thought.*

Several women's stories referenced fraternities, athletic teams, and other all-male peer groups. Although such groups may be associated with rape-prone cultures, they are also often controlled at multiple levels (by athletic departments, Greek life offices, national organizations, and others). Control and regulation means that students can be reached within their peer groups by requiring training sessions on consent, substance use, and responsibility, practices that are commonplace but not always required. Research has shown that rape-prevention programs aimed at college men

---

* Students could read, for example, about Lynn M. Phillips's conception of the "pleasing woman" and the "together woman" and be asked to consider how these mores may create a cultural paradox on campus as the pleasing woman meets men's desires in an "actively selfless" way and the together woman is a sexually empowered agent of her own desire pitting victimization and agency against one another.

on athletic teams and in fraternities can impact beliefs and intentions, making them potential sites for the development of rape-free cultural attitudes.[7] This is not to say that prevention and awareness-raising efforts should be targeted only to students who identify as male or should occur in gender-divided spaces. In fact, women's stories also show that just as there is a gender divide in perpetration, there is a gender divide in responses to disclosures. Students of all gender identities should receive compulsory training related to prevention and effective responses.[8]

Two characteristics of rape-prone cultures are (1) high levels of reported rape and (2) rape that is excused as a ceremonial expression of masculinity.[9] Prevalence studies have revealed high levels of rape on American college and university campuses, and although the ceremonial aspect may be disputed, research and student testimony make it difficult to deny that sexual violence is often excused. At the University, twenty-six undergraduate women came forward to share their stories, and all of them believed that there were high levels of sexual violence at their school. In the twenty-eight cases discussed (two women experienced more than one assault), no perpetrator was found responsible by the institution. Thus, national conversations and the interviews from the University both indicate that rape-prone cultures exist at colleges and universities in the United States.[10]

Talcott Parsons and Gerald Platt argued that institutions of higher education have significant influence on the culture of a society.[11] It follows that if we can change this campus culture, we can impact society at large. Peggy Reeves Sanday offers an alternative to the rape-prone culture—the rape-free culture. A "rape-free society is one in which the act of rape is either infrequent or does not occur. I used the term 'rape free' not to suggest that rape was entirely absent in a given society but as a label to indicate that sexual aggression is socially disapproved and punished severely."[12] If we take a two-pronged approach to shifting culture by (1) building empathy and understanding to increase social disapproval of sexual violence and (2) enacting policies that punish the crimes, we are likely to see reduced rates of sexual violence. Colleges and universities are a good place for this work because they are regulated spaces constructed to serve the public good and already have support systems in place. The work to shift institutional cultures is challenging, but critically engaging with the individuals who have experienced sexual violence on campus is a good place to start.

The women's stories shared in this book are authentic illustrations of the plurality of forms of agency used by college women in the time following experiences with campus sexual assault. In expanding the ways in which post-assault agency forms are used by women as well as their perceptions of their colleges in these moments of crisis, this project not only aids in the enhancement of institutional, state, and federal policies related to sexual violence, but it also contributes a counter-narrative or a narrative of resistance against the marginalization of women's actions and experiences. In explaining how they responded, women shift the paradigm of conversations about campus sexual violence from prescriptive and idealistic to descriptive and truthful. The operative question that can drive changes in the way that we think about campus sexual assault then becomes "what do women actually do?" rather than "what should they do?"

As we move forward, please remember Bettina, and how she was "paralyzed with fear" saying to herself, "it'll be over soon, it'll be over soon." Don't forget Alice listening to Zack ask if he should walk her home after raping her in his room. Recall the woman sitting in the scalding shower for twenty minutes thinking, "oh my god, oh my god" and praying that she would wake up and find that it was "the worst nightmare in the world." Think about Claire, sleeping on the floor beside her bed for several nights after being attacked and urinating in her sheets.

When people use or refer to a rape myth, remember that Diana behaved as she thought the "perfect victim" would—going to the emergency room, having a rape kit administered, speaking to the police, and pressing charges—and still felt that she was treated as a suspect and did not get the justice she sought.

Recall Diana, who listened to the student who assaulted her as he charmed the adjudication board into a not responsible finding.

Consider for a moment Eva, who thought she didn't deserve justice because she didn't make a public scene.

Think about Imogene, who still worries that the man who raped her will rape other women because, under pressure from her peers, she decided not to press charges or make a public statement in order to preserve the relationship between her sorority and the perpetrator's fraternity.

Imagine Naomi sitting in the back of a car driven by two fraternity members that she did not know, and Laura walking shoeless across campus. Picture Georgia cutting her hair, Tina writing a letter, and Uma photographing her bruises. Picture Olivia in the emergency room, holding onto her friend Jill's hand, and Penny waiting in the ER for three hours.

Reflect on a place where students say they might report sexual assault "if the school dealt with things differently." Because the statistics "are actually pretty horrific . . . not a single person has been suspended or expelled even when the panel found that they were guilty . . . so I could put myself through this absolutely horrific experience . . . and nothing has happened to him at all" and "cheat on an exam, and then you're kicked out . . . and you can rape someone and then it's like, 'see you on Monday.'"

Yet, at this same place, there is hope and empowerment. Consider the women who found other students, faculty, and staff who were trusted advisors and supporters. Think about Xena singing at the vigil and the woman who is out leading her peers in researching gender violence.

Most importantly, this project is about learning from Bettina who said, "I have the power to change this so I will do everything in my power to make sure this doesn't happen to somebody else."

Appendix A
Participant Demographics and Case Details

Total number of undergraduate participants=26
Total number of assaults described=28

Table A.1. Participants' Academic Year at Time of Interview

Academic year	N
Freshman	1
Sophomore	1
Junior	7
Senior	9
Fifth year	8

Note: Several of the fifth-year students were in their fifth year of study but did not identify as graduate students because they had taken time off following incidents of sexual assault and/or rape and had not yet graduated with bachelor's degrees at the time of the interview.

Table A.2. Participants' Academic Year at Time of Experience with Campus Sexual Violence

Academic year	N
Freshman	8
Sophomore	7
Junior	7
Senior	3
Fifth year	1
Other: During orientation	1
Other: Over the course of three years	1

Note: One woman experienced campus sexual violence twice and another experienced repeated violence over the course of three years.

Table A.3. Location of Sexual Violence

Location	N
On campus	10
Off campus proper, adjacent to campus	15
Studying abroad	1
Various locations (multiple assaults)	2

Table A.4. Participants' Described Knowledge of Perpetrator

Described knowledge of perpetrator	N
Friend (student)	10
Acquaintance (student)	7
Former romantic partner	6
Stranger (student)	3
Family member	1
Stranger (unidentified)	1

Appendix B
Methodological Notes

Appearance

The vignettes in this book omit physical descriptions of the women unless they were directly relevant to the story (for example, Georgia's hair was an important detail because she managed perceptions by cutting it). This was an intentional decision made not only because physical characteristics could reveal the identities of the women, but also because a historical analysis of print media coverage of campus sexual violence in the United States over the past twenty-five years revealed that women within a particular demographic group (namely white, upper-middle class, privileged females)[1] were more represented than any other group. I did not want to perpetuate the idea that appearance is important in cases of campus sexual assault, so I did not include physical descriptions of the women in the project.

References to Those "Accused" of Crimes

As I explained in chapter 1, I believed all of the women in the project. I sat in rooms with them as they shared their stories and I listened and I trusted them. Consequently, I refer to the *perpetrators* of the crimes, not the *accused*. If my belief alone isn't enough, note that research has shown that over a ten-year period only 5.9 percent of allegations at a "major Northeastern university" were false.[2] Additionally, this book is about the point of view and perceptions of the women who shared their stories. As a result, I do not refer to perpetrators as "accused" unless I am referencing a media story. No one is on trial in this book.

Substance Use

There are studies that have linked campus sexual assault to substance use. However, substance use was not a focus of many women's stories and, since the book is about what the women said, substance use plays a small part in this book.

Appendix C
Supplementary Ideas

Throughout this project, the women involved made suggestions for creating more effective programs and policies. Other ideas manifested in the analytic process. Although the primary recommendation of the book is to work to shift the culture on college and university campuses, these programmatic and/or pragmatic ideas may be useful.

- It is important for peers, family members, and other individuals to take note of behavioral shifts and follow up with those they care about. Conversely, it is worth remembering that late adolescence is often a time of identity exploration. Changes may not signal anything, but they are a good point for starting a conversation.
- Institutions and students could benefit from transparency about the processes for taking time off and what effect this may have on GPAs and tracking. Because students worry about how faculty will perceive them if they disclose a sexual assault incident, institutions should provide faculty and staff development around student needs and encourage transparency in all dealings.
- Since women frequently disclosed incidents of sexual assault to peers and a range of peer responses were useful to them, basic attending skills could be taught, modeled, and practiced at orientation and revisited throughout the college experience.
- Peers inadvertently (or at least it was perceived as non-intentional) intervened by entering spaces or making sounds, but there were very few cases of active bystander intervention among the stories shared in this project. This may have been because peers did not see or know what was going on, but it underscores the need for training peers.
- Conversations about expectations and consent should be discussed with *all* students. Greater emphasis on training, particularly non-gendered and equal training, is critically important.
- A major challenge to dealing with the aftermath of campus sexual violence is, in many cases, proximity or perceived proximity. A primary concern was enrolling in a class with the perpetrator and being surprised on the first day when he was there. While it would take conversations about the applications of FERPA, it is worth considering a process where women who report incidents (whether or not they want to press charges) can be notified if they are enrolling in the same class as a perpetrator. Interim measures of this sort exist on come campuses and in general women felt that they would ease anxiety.
- Family members may want to educate themselves and have conversations with their students, regardless of their gender identity, so that students know that they will be believed and supported if something *does* happen to them. More positively, families can work toward prevention by more readily having open conversations about consent and respect regardless of context.

- Georgia spoke about the importance of having a coach that she knew would believe and support her. Another woman talked about a person who worked with her student organization to whom she disclosed. On campuses where large classes are the norm, advisors to social groups can be very important. Learning communities may be one way to connect *all* students to faculty and staff on a consistent, longitudinal basis.

- Being attacked can take away a sense of power and control. It is not surprising, then, that many women seek a sense of control in the aftermath of sexual violence. When considering formal justice-seeking mechanisms such as pressing charges through institutional adjudication boards, women may believe they will not have control over the process or input in the outcome. Women shared that they worried that the consequences for sexual assault were not necessarily aligned with what they saw as appropriate. Institutions should consider tiered penalty systems wherein women can examine a range of potential penalties and have some say in how the process proceeds.

- Some women found healing through artistic expression (writing, blogging, music, etc.) and others through working out. Students and colleges should construct outlets including art shows, writing groups, yoga classes, and other experientially based groups for people who have faced campus sexual assault. For example, the school could host an art show where submissions related to a theme around agency after and prevention of sexual assault can be entered with or without a name. This would not only give an outlet for artistic expression and empowerment, but it would also educate others and be a place where information and referral materials could be available. Such a program might also highlight the multiplicity of pathways toward healing available to women and encourage identification with agent status among students.

- Women who spoke about empowerment can also be a substantial resource for administrators and policy makers. For example, they can sit on advisory councils and/or participate in focus groups about potential interventions and service provisions. They could (and some do) serve as resources for other women who have experienced campus sexual violence. Additionally, their post-assault stories and pathways could be shared and compiled as a resource for others considering post-assault options. Their stories could also be used as tools to build empathy among other members of student bodies. I strongly recommend local level story gathering to give survivors a platform for empowerment and to build an authentic sense of empathy.

Notes

Preface

1. Ahearn 2001, 112.
2. Koss, Gidycz, and Wisniewski 1987, 169.
3. Herman 1997, 1.

Acknowledgments

1. "Make Them Hear You" is from the musical *Ragtime* as recorded in 1998. Lyrics by Lynn Ahrens. Music by Stephen Flaherty. Copyright © 1996 WB Music Corp., Pen and Perseverence and Hillsdale Music, Inc. All rights administered by WB Music Corp. All rights reserved. Used by permission of Alfred Music.

Chapter 1. What We Don't Know about Campus Sexual Assault

1. Jones 2014; Tucker 2014; Seawell and Ekpo 2014; O'Gorman Hughes and Sandler 1987.
2. Headlines from Bogdanich 2014; Carmody 1989; Flint 1989; Weiss 2014; Wynter 1988; Anderson 2014.
3. Office of the Vice-President 2014.
4. Stone 2002, 163, 167–68.
5. Kirkpatrick and Kanin 1957, 57.
6. Koss and Gidycz 1985; Koss and Oros 1982; Koss, Gidycz, and Wisniewski 1987, 169.
7. Fisher, Cullen, and Turner 2000, 10.
8. Krebs et al. 2007.
9. *Animal House* 1978.
10. Barnett and Feild 1977; Coller and Resick 1987; Muehlenhard 1988; Holcomb et al. 1991; Burd 1999; Lonsway and Fitzgerald 1994; Muehlenhard and Linton 1987; Warshaw 1994, 20.
11. Feild 1978; Barnett and Feild 1977; Harrison, Downes, and Williams 1991; Holcomb et al. 1991; Krebs et al. 2007.
12. Hinch and Thomas 1999, 795.
13. Marcus 1992, 390–91.
14. Mardorossian 2002.
15. Littleton et al. 2009; Mohler-Kuo et al. 2004; Tyler, Hoyt, and Whitbeck 1998; Krebs et al. 2007; Undercover colors: http://www.undercovercolors.com.
16. Hinch and Thomas 1999. For examples of studies that have linked campus sexual violence to substance use see Mohler-Kuo et al. 2004; Tyler, Hoyt, and Whitbeck 1998; and Krebs et al. 2007.
17. Sanday 1996, 193; Smith 2014; Pérez-Peña and Bogdanich 2014.
18. Office of the Vice-President 2014, ii.

19. For a full listing of related federal legislation visit http://clerycenter.org/policy -accomplishments.

20. The site knowyourix.org contains more information about Title IX.

21. See http://www.huffingtonpost.com/2015/04/06/colleges-federal-investigation -title-ix-106_n_7011422.html. The group Know Your IX is a great resource.

22. Brozan 1986; Ehrhart and Sandler 1985.

23. Flint 1989; Koss, Gidycz, and Wisniewski 1987, 20.

24. Stone 2002, 213

25. Janosik and Gregory 2003.

26. Fisher et al. 2002.

27. Janosik 2001, 357; Colaner 2006; Nicklin 1999.

28. Office of the Vice-President 2014, 3.

29. Fisher et al. 2003.

30. Herman 1997, 2.

31. Oakley 1981; Paget 1983.

32. Millar 1998, 200.

33. Creese 2011, 52–53.

34. DeVault and Gross 2007; Lisak et al. 2010, 1318.

35. There are many statistics with citations available at http://www.oneinfourusa .org/statistics.php. Some include: (1) "For female rape survivors, 98.1% of the time a man was the perpetrator (Black et al. 2011); (2) For male rape survivors, 93% of the time, a man was the perpetrator (Black et al. 2011); (3) Two different longitudinal studies have found that fraternity men are three times more likely to commit sexual assault than other college men (Foubert, Newberry, and Tatum 2007; Loh et al. 2005); and (4) Rapists are almost always (98%) men (Sedgwick 2006).

Chapter 2. The Paradox of Embodied Agency

1. For studies that support the assertion that most college students are assaulted by acquaintances, see Flack et al. 2008; Ullman, Karabatsos, and Koss 1999; and Krebs et al. 2007.

2. The words that appear in quotes came directly from a 2013 email sent to college students at a university in the United States and the rest of the suggestions are derived from other campus emails.

3. Projansky 2001, 109.

4. Slaughter et al. 1997, 612.

5. Lott, Reily, and Froward 1982.

6. Gavey 1998, 24.

Chapter 3. Managing Identity

1. Herman 1997, 53.

2. http://dictionary.reference.com/browse/homeostasis?s=t

3. Lott, Reily, and Froward 1982; Flack et al. 2008; Ullman, Karabatsos, and Koss 1999.

Chapter 4. Telling Friends and Family

1. http://www.merriam-webster.com/dictionary/say; Rogers 2007, 44.

2. In a 2003 study, Fisher and colleagues reported that 90 percent of the participants in the National College Women Sexual Victimization (NCWSV) study disclosed the incident to a friend (Fisher et al. 2003) and in a 2007 study conducted by Ahrens and colleagues it was reported that nearly 75 percent of survivors told an "informal support provider" (Ahrens et al. 2007).

3. Ahrens et al. 2007, 46.

4. For a study that found stranger rape more likely to be reported than acquaintance rape, see Lott, Reily, and Froward 1982.

5. Herman 1997, 7.

Chapter 5. Seeking Justice

1. Seawell and Ekpo 2014.

2. Bogdanich 2014.

3. Arditi 2014. For a public statement from Lena Sclove see https://www.youtube .com/watch?v=xA-EGAlhJoE; for a written statement from Daniel Kopin see http://www .documentcloud.org/documents/1149238-daniel-kopin-statement.html.

4. Lamb 2014.

5. Warshaw 1994, 20.

Chapter 7. Agency and Campus Sexual Assault: The Way Forward

1. U.S. Senate Subcommittee on Financial and Contracting Oversight 2014, 1.

2. van Dijk 2009, 6.

3. Ibid., 2.

4. Barnett and Feild 1977.

5. Koneru 2014.

6. U.S. Senate Subcommittee on Financial and Contracting Oversight 2014, 1.

7. For examples see Foubert and Newberry 2006 and Foubert and Perry 2007.

8. The concept of a rape-prone campus culture comes from Sanday 1996.

9. Sanday 1981.

10. Sanday 1996; Krebs et al. 2007. For recent research see U.S. Senate Subcommittee on Financial and Contracting Oversight 2014. For examples of student testimonies see Smith 2014 and Bogdanich 2014.

11. Parsons and Platt 1973.

12. Sanday 1996, 191–92.

Appendix B. Methodological Notes

1. For examples, see the photos associated with these stories in Rule 1989 and Schreiber 1990.

2. Lisak et al. 2010.

Bibliography

Abbey, A., P. McAuslan, and L. T. Ross. 1998. "Sexual Assault Perpetration by College Men: The Role of Alcohol, Misperception of Sexual Intent, and Sexual Beliefs and Experiences." *Journal of Social and Clinical Psychology* 17: 167–95.

Ahearn, L. M. 2001. "Language and Agency." *Annual Review of Anthropology* 30: 109–37.

Ahrens, C. E., G. Cabral, and S. Abeling. 2009. "Healing or Hurtful: Sexual Assault Survivors' Interpretations of Social Reactions from Support Providers." *Psychology of Women Quarterly* 33: 81–94.

Ahrens, C. E., and R. Campbell. 2000. "Assisting Rape Victims as They Recover from Rape: The Impact on Friends." *Journal of Interpersonal Violence* 15, no. 9: 959–86. doi:10.1177/088626000015009004.

Ahrens, C. E., R. Campbell, N. K. Ternier-Thames, S. M. Wasco, and T. Sefl. 2007. "Deciding Whom to Tell: Expectations and Outcomes of Rape Survivors' First Disclosures." *Psychology of Women Quarterly* 31, no. 1: 38–49. doi:10.1111/j.1471-6402.2007.00329.

Anderson, N. 2014. "How Colleges Vary in Reports of Sex Assault and Other Sex Offenses." *Washington Post*, June 29. http://www.washingtonpost.com/local/education/how-colleges-vary-in-reports-of-sex-assault-and-other-sex-offenses/2014/06/29/a8d9cc00-fe09-11e3-8176-f2c941cf35f1_story.html.

Animal House (motion picture). 1978. Directed by J. Landis. United States, Universal Studios.

Arditi, L. 2014. "Brown Student Accused of 'Sexual Misconduct' Says He Won't Return to Campus in the Fall." *Providence Journal*, April 26. http://www.providencejournal.com/news/police-fire/20140426-brown-student-accused-of-sexual-misconduct-says-he-wont-return-to-campus-in-the-fall.ece.

Barnett, N. J., and H. S. Feild. 1977. "Sex Differences in University Students' Attitudes towards Rape." *Journal of College Student Personnel* 2: 93–96.

Bergquist, W. H., and K. Pawlak. 2008. *Engaging the Six Cultures of the Academy*. San Francisco, CA: Jossey-Bass.

Black, M. C., K. C. Basile, M. J. Breiding, S. G. Smith, M. L. Walters, M. T. Merrick, J. Chen, and M. R. Stevens. 2011. *The National Intimate Partner and Sexual Violence Survey (NISVS): 2010 Summary Report*. Atlanta, GA: National Center for Injury Prevention and Control, Centers for Disease Control and Prevention.

Bogdanich, W. 2014. "Reporting Rape, and Wishing She Hadn't: How One College Handled a Sexual Assault Complaint." *New York Times*, July 12. http://www.nytimes.com/2014/07/13/us/how-one-college-handled-a-sexual-assault-complaint.html?_r=0.

Brown, B. 2010. "Brené Brown: The Power of Vulnerability." (Video file: June). Retrieved from: http://www.ted.com/talks/brene_brown_on_vulnerability?language=e.

Brozan, N. 1986. "Gang Rape: A Rising Campus Concern," *New York Times*, February 17, B8.

Burd, S. 1999. "Incidents That Are Not Reported to Police Remain a Thorny Issue in Crime Reports." *Chronicle of Higher Education*, May 28, A42.

Carmody, D. 1989. "Increasing Rapes on Campus Spur Colleges to Fight Back," *New York Times*, January 1, sec. 1, p. 1.

Clark, M. 2014. *College Sexual Assault: A Campus-By-Campus Report Card*. msnbc.com, August 26. http://www.msnbc.com/ronan-farrow-daily/college-sexual-assault-campus-campus-report-card.

Colaner, K. T. 2006. "Towards Greater Campus Safety: An Examination of Student Affairs Administrators' Knowledge of and Compliance with the Clery Act." PhD diss., Rossier School of Education, University of Southern California.

Coller, S. A., and P. A. Resick. 1987. "Women's Attributions of Responsibility for Date Rape: The Influence of Empathy and Sex-Role Stereotyping." *Violence and Victims* 2, no. 2: 115–25.

Creese, A. 2011. "Making Local Practices Globally Relevant in Researching Multilingual Education." In *Educational Linguistics in Practice: Applying the Local Globally and the Global Locally*, edited by F. M. Hult and K. A. King, 41–58. Tonawanda, NY: Multilingual Matters.

DeVault, M. L., and G. Gross. 2007. "Feminist Interviewing: Experience, Talk and Knowledge." In *Handbook of Feminist Research*, edited by S. N. Hesse-Biber, 173–97. Thousand Oaks, CA: Sage Publications.

Ehrhart, J. K., and B. R. Sandler. 1985. "Campus Gang Rape: Party Games?" Association of American Colleges, Project on the Status and Education of Women (November).

Erikson, F. 2009. "Four Points Concerning Policy-Oriented Qualitative Research." In *Qualitative Inquiry and Social Justice: Toward a Politics of Hope*, edited by N. K. Denzin and M. D. Giardina, 73–80. Walnut Creek, CA: Left Coast Press.

Feild, H. S. 1978. "Attitudes toward Rape: A Comparative Analysis of Police, Rapists, Crisis Counselors, and Citizens. *Journal of Personality and Social Psychology* 36, no. 2: 156–79.

Fisher, B. S., F. T. Cullen, and M. G. Turner. 2000. *The Sexual Victimization of College Women*. Washington, DC: U.S. Department of Justice.

Fisher, B. S., L. E. Daigle, F. T. Cullen, and M. G. Turner. 2003. "Reporting Sexual Victimization to the Police and Others: Results from a National-Level Study of College Women." *Criminal Justice and Behavior* 30, no. 1: 6–38.

Fisher, B. S., J. L. Hartman, F. T. Cullen, and M. G. Turner. 2002. "Making Campuses Safer for Students: The Clery Act as a Symbolic Legal Reform." *Stetson Law Review* 32: 61–89.

Flack, W. F., M. L. Caron, S. J. Leinen, K. G. Breitenbach, A. M. Barber, E. N. Brown, C. T. Gilbert, T. F. Harchak, M. M. Hendricks, C. E. Rector, H. T. Schatten, and H. C. Stein. 2008. "'The Red Zone:' Temporal Risk for Unwanted Sex Among College Students." *Journal of Interpersonal Violence* 23, no. 9: 1177–96. doi: 10.1177/088626050831430.

Flint, A. 1989. "Lawsuits New Weapon against Campus Rape." *Boston Globe*, September 25, National/Foreign, p. 1.

Foubert, J. D., and J. T. Newberry. 2006. "Effects of Two Versions of an Empathy-Based Rape Prevention Program on Fraternity Men's Rape Survivor Empathy, Rape Myth Acceptance, Likelihood of Raping, and Likelihood of Committing Sexual Assault." *Journal of College Student Development* 47: 133–48.

Foubert, J. D., J. T. Newberry, and J. L. Tatum. 2007. "Behavior Differences Seven Months Later: Effects of a Rape Prevention Program on First-Year Men Who Join Fraternities." *Journal of Student Affairs Research and Practice* 44: 728–49.

Foubert, J. D., and B. C. Perry. 2007. "Creating Lasting Attitude and Behavior Change in Fraternity Members and Male Student Athletes." *Violence against Women* 13: 70–86.

Gavey, N. 1998. *Just Sex? The Cultural Scaffolding of Rape.* New York: Routledge.

Harrison, P. J., J. Downes, and M. D. Williams. 1991. "Date and Acquaintance Rape: Perceptions and Attitude Change Strategies." *Journal of College Student Development* 32: 131–39.

Heberle, R. 2000. "Victimization and Consent." *Hypatia* 17: 257–64. doi:10.1111/j.1527 -2001.2002.tb00954.x.

Herman, J. 1997. *Trauma and Recovery: The Aftermath of Violence—from Domestic Abuse to Political Terror.* New York: Basic Books.

Hinch, S. S., and R. W. Thomas. 1999. "Rape Myth Acceptance and College Students: How Far We Have Come." *Sex Roles: A Journal of Research*, 815–32.

Holcomb, D. R., L. Holcomb, K. A. Sondag, and N. Williams. 1991. "Attitudes about Date Rape: Gender Differences among College Students." *College Student Journal* 25: 434–39.

Janosik, S. M. 2001. "The Impact of the Campus Crime Awareness Act on Student Behavior." *NASPA Journal* 38, no. 3: 348–60.

Janosik, S. M., and D. E. Gregory. 2003. "The Clery Act and Its Influence on Campus Law Enforcement Practices." *NASPA Journal* 41, no. 1: 182–99.

Jones, J. H. 2014. "Students Rally against Rape at CSUSM." *U-T San Diego*, August 26. http://www.utsandiego.com/news/2014/aug/26/rape-san-marcos-university-rally -fraternity/.

Kirkpatrick, C., and E. Kanin. 1957. "Male Sex Aggression on a University Campus." *American Sociological Review* 22: 52–58.

Klonsky, E. D. 2007. "Non-Suicidal Self-Injury: An Introduction," *Journal of Clinical Psychology* 63, no. 11: 1039. doi:10.1002/jclp.20411, PMID 17932979.

Koneru, C. K. 2014. "Sexual Assault on College Campuses: The Need for Federal Legislation." *NC Policy Watch*, September 10. http://www.ncpolicywatch.com/2014/09/10/sexual -assault-on-college-campuses-the-need-for-federal-legislation/#sthash.nCKNu31U .yHTl6NA9.dpuf.

Koss, M. P., and C. A. Gidycz. 1985. "Sexual Experiences Survey: Reliability and Validity." *Journal of Consulting and Clinical Psychology* 53: 422–23.

Koss, M. P., C. A. Gidycz, and N. Wisniewski. 1987. "The Scope of Rape: Incidence and Prevalence of Sexual Aggression and Victimization in a National Sample of Higher Education Students." *Journal of Consulting and Clinical Psychology* 55, no. 2: 162–70.

Koss, M. P., and C. J. Oros. 1982. "Sexual Experiences Survey: A Research Instrument Investigating Sexual Aggression and Victimization." *Journal of Consulting and Clinical Psychology* 50: 455–57.

Krebs, C. P., C. H. Lindquist, T. D. Warner, B. S. Fisher, and S. L. Martin. 2007. *The Campus Sexual Assault Study.* (NIJ Document No. 221153). http://www.ncjrs.gov/pdffiles1/nij /grants/221153.pdf.

Lamb, K. 2014. "U. Mishandled Sexual Assault Case Victim Says." *Brown Daily Herald*, April 23. http://www.browndailyherald.com/2014/04/23/u-mishandled-sexual-assault-case-victim-says/.

Lisak, D., L. Gardinier, S. C. Nicksa, and A. M. Cote. 2010. "False Allegations of Sexual Assault: An Analysis of Ten Years of Reported Cases." *Violence against Women* 16, no. 12: 1318–34. doi: 10.1177/1077801210387747.

Littleton, H., H. Tabernik, E. J. Canales, and T. Backstrom. 2009. "Risky Situation or Harmless Fun? A Qualitative Examination of College Women's Bad Hook-up and Rape Scripts." *Sex Role* 60, no. 11–12: 793–804. doi: 10.1007/s11199-009-9586-8.

Loh, C., C. A. Gidycz, T. R. Lobo, and R. Luthra. 2005. "A Prospective Analysis of Sexual Assault Perpetration: Risk Factors Related to Perpetrator Characteristics." *Journal of Interpersonal Violence* 20, no. 10 (October): 1325–48. doi: 10.1177/0886260505278528.

Lonsway, L. A., and L. F. Fitzgerald. 1994. "Rape myths: In Review." *Psychology of Women Quarterly* 18: 133–64.

Lott, B., M. Reily, and D. Froward. 1982. "Sexual Assault and Harassment: A Campus Community Case Study." *Journal of Women in Culture and Society* 8, no. 2: 296–319.

Marcus, S. 1992. "Fighting Bodies, Fighting Words: A Theory and Politics of Rape Prevention." In *Feminists Theorize the Political*, edited by J. Butler and J. W. Scott, 385–403. New York: Routledge.

Mardorossian, C. M. 2002. "Toward a New Feminist Theory of Rape." *Signs: Journal of Women in Culture and Society* 27, no. 3: 743–75.

Millar, M. S. 1998. *Cracking the Gender Code: Who Rules the Wired World?* Toronto, ON: Second Story Press.

Mohler-Kuo, M., G. W. Dowdall, M. P. Koss, and H. Wechsler. 2004. "Correlates of Rape While Intoxicated in a National Sample of College Women." *Journal of Studies on Alcohol* 65, no. 1: 37–45.

Muehlenhard, C. L. 1988. "'Nice Women' Don't Say Yes and 'Real Men' Don't Say No: How Miscommunication and the Sexual Double Standard Can Cause Sexual Problems." *Women and Therapy* 7: 95–108.

Muehlenhard, C. L., and M. A. Linton. 1987. "Date Rape and Sexual Aggression in Dating Situations: Incidence and Risk Factors." *Journal of Counseling Psychology* 34: 186–96.

Nicklin, J. L. 1999. "Colleges Differ Widely on How They Tally Incidents under Crime-Reporting Law." *Chronicle of Higher Education*, May 28, A41–42.

Oakley, A. 1981. "Interviewing Women: A Contradiction in Terms." In *Doing Feminist Research*, edited by H. Roberts, pp. 30–61. London: Routledge & Kegan Paul.

Office of the Vice-President and The White House Council on Women and Girls. 2014. *Not Alone: The First Report of the White House Task Force to Protect Students From Sexual Assault*. https://www.notalone.gov/assets/report.pdf.

O'Gorman Hughes, J., and B. R. Sandler. 1987. *"Friends" Raping Friends: Could It Happen to You?* Washington, DC: Project on the Status and Education of Women, Association of American Colleges.

Paget, M. A. 1983. "Experience and Knowledge." *Human Studies* 6, no. 1: 67–90. doi: 10.1007/BF0212777.

Parsons, T., and G. Platt. 1973. *The American University*. Cambridge, MA: Harvard University Press.

Pérez-Peña, R., and W. Bogdanich. 2014. "In Florida Student Assaults, an Added Burden on Accusers." *New York Times,* September 14.

Philips, L. M. 2000. *Flirting with Danger: Young Women's Reflections on Sexuality and Domination.* New York: New York University Press.

Projansky, S. 2001. *Watching Rape: Film and Television in Postfeminist Culture.* New York: New York University Press.

Pusser, B., and S. Marginson. 2011. "The Elephant in the Room: Power, Global Rankings, and the Study of Higher Education Organizations." In *The Organization of Higher Education: Managing Colleges for a New Era,* edited by M. N. Bastedo. Baltimore: Johns Hopkins University Press.

Rogers, A. 2007. *The Unsayable: The Hidden Language of Trauma.* New York: Ballantine Books.

Rule, A. 1989. "Rape on Campus." *Good Housekeeping,* September 1, 209.

Sanday, P. R. 1981. "The Socio-Cultural Context of Rape: A Cross-Cultural Study." *Journal of Social Issues* 37, no. 4: 5–27.

Sanday, P. R. 1996. "Rape-Prone versus Rape-Free Campus Cultures." *Violence against Women* 2, no. 2: 191–208.

Schreiber, L. A. 1990. "The Glamour Report: Campus Rape," *Glamour* (September): 288–93.

Seawell, S., and P. Ekpo. 2014. "'Rape List' Returns: 25 Years of Sexual Assault Activism at Brown." *Bluestockings Magazine* (May 15). http://bluestockingsmag.com/2014/05/15/rape-list-returns-25-years-of-sexual-assault-activism-at-brown/.

Sedgwick, J. L. 2006. *Criminal Victimization in the United States, 2005 Statistical Tables: National Crime Victimization Survey.* Washington, DC: U.S. Department of Justice, Bureau of Justice Statistics. NCJ 215244.

Slaughter, L., C.R.V. Brown, S. Crowley, and R. Peck. 1997. "Patterns of Genital Injury in Female Sexual Assault Victims." *American Journal of Obstetrics and Gynecology* 176: 609.

Smith, R. 2014. "In a Mattress, a Lever for Art and Political Protest." *New York Times,* September 21. http://www.nytimes.com/2014/09/22/arts/design/in-a-mattress-a-fulcrum-of-art-and-political-protest.html.

Stone, D. 2002. *Policy Paradox: The Art of Political Decision Making.* New York: W.W. Norton.

Testa, M., J. A. Livingston, and R. L. Collins. 2000. "The Role of Women's Alcohol Consumption in Evaluation of Vulnerability to Sexual Aggression." *Experimental and Clinical Psychopharmacology* 8, no. 2: 185–91.

Tucker, C. 2014. "UNCG Students March to Protest Sexual Assaults on College Campuses Nationwide." Fox 8 WGHB, August 27. http://myfox8.com/2014/08/27/uncg-students-march-to-protest-sexual-assaults-on-college-campuses-nationwide/.

Tyler, K. A., D. R. Hoyt, and L. B. Whitbeck. 1998. "Coercive Sexual Strategies." *Violence and Victims* 13, no. 1: 47–61.

Ullman, S. E., G. Karabatsos, and M. P. Koss. 1999. "Alcohol and Sexual Assault in a National Sample of College Women." *Journal of Interpersonal Violence* 14, no. 6: 603–25. doi: 10.1177/088626099014006003.

U.S. Senate Subcommittee on Financial and Contracting Oversight. 2014. *Sexual Violence on Campus: How Too Many Institutions Are Failing to Protect Students.* http://www.mccaskill.senate.gov/SurveyReportwithAppendix.pdf.

van Dijk, J. M. 2009. "Free the Victim: A Critique of the Western Conception of Victim-hood." *The International Review of Victimology* 16, no. 1: 1–33.

Warshaw, R. 1994. *I Never Called It Rape*. New York: Harper Perennial.

Weiss, J. 2014. "To Prevent Sexual Assault, Appeal to Peer Pressure." *Boston Globe*, August 31. http://www.bostonglobe.com/opinion/2014/08/30/affirmative-consent -prevent-sexual-assault-appeal-peer-pressure instead/wrlqoXRXEiNyiQyzNXQV4J /story.html.

Wynter, L. 1988. "Campus Rapes Create Alarm at College Park." *Washington Post*, November 13, MD: 1. Database online, available from ProQuest Historical Newspapers.

Index